Choices in Caring

CONTEMPORARY APPROACHES TO CHILD AND YOUTH CARE WORK

Mark A. Krueger
Norman W. Powell
Editors

Child Welfare League of America • Washington, DC

CHILD WELFARE LEAGUE OF AMERICA, INC.
440 First Street, NW, Suite 310, Washington, DC 20001-2085

CURRENT PRINTING (last digit)
10 9 8 7 6 5 4 3 2 1

Cover and text design by Kevin Erskine

Printed in the United States of America

ISBN # 0-87868-376-3

TO

Fritz Redl
Al Trieschman
Ola
and
Bobby

Contents

Foreword

Fritz Redl was an internationally acclaimed scholar and clinician who cared about aggressive delinquent children. He was their friend and mentor, with great insights into the complexity of helping them. Redl understood the nature of their early developmental deprivation, the destructive power of their social reality, and the frequency of physical and psychological conflicts they experienced in their daily activities at home, in school, and on the streets. As Redl studied the problems of treating these resistant children who were in the juvenile justice or the mental health system, he concluded that the use of individual psychotherapy, by itself, was not powerful enough to make a difference in their lives. Redl's response to this treatment problem was to expand the concept of the treatment team to include all the staff members who worked and lived with these children every day. This meant reaching out and providing training for more skills to child care workers, hospital attendants, classroom teachers, recreational leaders, probation officers, and other community and residential workers.

In 1952, Redl documented and promoted his new total treatment philosophy by publishing, with David Wineman, two now classic books entitled *Children Who Hate* and *Controls From Within*. These books, which were based on Redl's clinical and educational treatment program with delinquent boys at Pioneer House in Detroit, presented the helping professions with a host of new, exciting, and effective therapeutic concepts and intervention skills, such as The Therapeutic Milieu; Seventeen Management Techniques; Life Space Interviewing; The Meaning of Punishment; The Dynamics of Group Life; and The Significance of a Therapeutic Relationship. These concepts and skills were embraced enthusiastically by Redl's colleagues, and by 1960 they were adopted and incorporated into the basic training curriculum for graduate students wanting to work with these children. It was amazing how this one man, Fritz Redl, was able to bridge and unite the fields of special education, social work, clinical psychology, child psychiatry, and child care counseling through the elaboration of his concepts.

It was amazing how this one man's treatment philosophy significantly changed the ways in which professionals approached and helped these troubled children.

Redl's time was a creative time, a time of growing professional optimism, program innovation, and expanding treatment services. Thirty-five years later, the concepts remain, even though the professional optimism has faded. Redl died in February 1988, but not before he commented on the changes in our society and discussed the current status of high-risk children. He talked about the multiplying number of urban gangs; the increase in poverty among minority children; the increase in violent delinquent acts; the drug wars; the sexual exploitation of children; the rapid rise in the number of homeless, abused, neglected, disappearing, and alcoholic children; and the shocking frequency of adolescent suicides and severe mental illness. He also reflected on the marginal school programs for these children, the lack of group homes, and the exorbitant cost of residential care. At the end of this conversation Redl shook his head and said, sadly: "All of a sudden, in today's society, we have to *prove* that somebody ought to take care of our children. This is a frightening thought!"

For a man who had dedicated his life to caring for these children, it was painful to acknowledge the changes in society, and the deep and pervasive negative attitudes our citizens have toward helping troubled children and youths. As a result, new policies, programs, and resources will not be developed for these children unless new leaders emerge in the field to challenge public apathy and resistance to caring for these children.

With the publishing of this book, *Choices in Caring*, the new professional leaders from the field of child care counseling have identified themselves. Mark Krueger and Norman Powell are young and talented, experienced and skilled professionals, who are dedicated to enhancing the quality of caring of future child care counselors. They have taken the concepts and contributions of Fritz Redl and his followers, such as Henry Maier, Al Trieschman, James Whittaker, Larry Brendtro, Arnold Goldstein, and Nicholas Hobbs, and they have built a new foundation of hope for troubled children.

Each chapter in this book defines and develops an important concept that is critical to the competency of a child care counselor. Whether the chapter is on child care organizations, the Conflict Cycle, or cross-cultural issues, the material is well written, realistic, and informative. *Choices in Caring* is a needed and important contribution to the field. It is a book that I enjoyed reading, and that Fritz Redl would have applauded.

Nicholas J. Long, Ph.D.
American University, Washington, DC

Preface

A child care worker was asked to describe his job. He responded:

> It's about choices. First we decide that we want to become involved in...building relationships with children. Then we decide how we're going to teach them the ABCs and DLRs [daily living routines]; how we're going to tuck them in and help them solve problems; how we're going to deal with temper tantrums, and so on. But in the end, they have to make choices about how they want to live. After they get to know and maybe like us, after they hopefully see and feel another side of themselves, they have to choose what they want to do with their lives. The most we can ultimately hope for is that they make better choices for themselves. It's as simple or perhaps as complex as that.

We have chosen the title, *Choices in Caring: Contemporary Approaches to Child and Youth Care Work*, because we agree with this worker; child and youth care work is largely about choices. Choices that we make when we enter the field. Choices that we make when we select a certain intervention strategy or philosophy of treatment. And most important, the constructive choices that we hope our children will be empowered to make after they have been in our care.

These are all tough, difficult, and demanding choices. They stretch the human fiber to its limit, not only because young lives hang in the balance but because we also have to strive to make each decision in a caring way, with empathy, compassion, trust, and security foremost in our minds.

Choices in child and youth care work also have to be made with the knowledge that the future of our society is inextricably linked with the destiny of our children. Caring for children is not a societal option. If our society does not begin to make a more serious effort to confront the problems that plague our troubled children, the quality of life in the future for us and our children will be in question.

Rollo May wrote in *The Courage to Create*, "A man or woman becomes fully human only by his or her choices and his or her commitment to them." The approaches that we have selected for this book reflect this attitude. Each contributor has based his or her approach on a conviction to enhance the quality of care for troubled children. Our philosophies and methods vary somewhat, but we all share a common commitment to serving the best interests of children and their families in today's complex society. This shared commitment includes a continued striving to recognize each child as a unique individual who has dignity and potential and who requires nurturing and encouragement. In our view, emotional disturbances, cultural differences, behavioral problems, and developmental delays are not handicaps but special starting places from which to build.

We see child and youth care workers primarily as teachers of the necessary daily life skills of social and emotional competence. This teaching is done through the therapeutic use of a meaningful relationship and constructive adult modeling. Child and youth care workers are at times also scientists, artisans, and artists. As scientists, they conduct their practices with technical rigor and a constant search for appropriate answers. As artisans, they hone their skills through hard work and hours of practice. And finally, as artists, they draw upon their intuitive talents to foster dynamic learning environments.

For the purposes of this book, child and youth care workers are defined as persons who work directly with troubled (emotionally disturbed, abused, chemically dependent, dependent neglected, delinquent, etc.) and/or developmentally handicapped (mentally retarded, physically impaired, deaf, blind, autistic, mentally ill, etc.) children and youths in residential treatment centers, group homes, temporary shelter care, psychiatric hospitals, correctional facilities, and home- and community-based programs.

The concepts presented here are based primarily on our group care experiences. We believe, however, that many of these ideas will be valuable to professionals in other settings.

Each chapter opens with a vignette that describes an incident from the writer's experience that is representative of the material that follows. There are six chapters in all. In the first chapter, "Child and Youth Care Organizations," Mark Krueger defines the tenets and organizational process that he believes guide contemporary child and youth care agencies. Next, Norman Powell explains how the "Conflict Cycle," a treatment model developed by special educator Nicholas Long, can be applied to contemporary child and youth care work. In chapter 3, "Social Skills Training: Teaching Troubled Youths To Be Socially Competent," Richard Fox describes in practical terms the principles and applications of a competency-based approach.

Gary Weaver, in chapter 4, "The Crisis of Cross-Cultural Child and Youth Care," vividly focuses attention on the importance of cross-cultural sensitivity and understanding. In chapter 5, "Child and Youth Care Work with the Deaf: An Orientation," George Cohen introduces members of the general child care community to child care work with the deaf, and shows how fundamental child and youth care concepts can be universally applied with both hearing and nonhearing children. Thom Garfat's closing chapter, "The Involvement of Family Members as Consumers in Treatment Programs for Troubled Youths," offers a new way of looking at family involvement.

We have all been there, on the line working directly with children and their families. Like a growing number of career-minded workers in this field, we have taken on responsibilities as consultants, program developers, educators, and administrators, but we have maintained our advocacy, enthusiasm, and support for child and youth care work. We hope that this devotion to the field is evident in our writing.

Acknowledgments

Our thanks and appreciation to:

Nick Long, Sue Pratt, and *Robert Martin*, for their constructive critique, continuous support, and valued friendship throughout this project;

Erika Hupperts for an original reading and editing of the chapters;

Cathie Sanders for typing and retyping as we made changes;

The CWLA Publications staff for being so friendly and supportive;

Carl Schoenberg for making it all read well;

and

Our colleagues in child and youth care who make it all work.

I

Child and Youth Care Organizations

Mark A. Krueger

My introduction to child care work was swift and abrupt. I arrived at 6:45 A.M. on my first day and walked to the second floor of the treatment center where I was greeted by several emotionally disturbed boys ages nine to 16. After telling them that I was new and could not answer their requests for toothbrushes and sheets, and fumbling my way through a few nasty comments and threats from them, I went into the child care office where I found my colleagues having a last cup of coffee. We introduced ourselves and then divvied up the children and tasks according to a formula that seemed both familiar and frustrating to the workers. Eva would put away linen. Nick would take the eight boys on the west end of the hall, I had the nine boys on the east end, and so on. Then we went off to get the children dressed and ready for school, tasks that I had absolutely no preparation for, and for which my colleagues were unable to offer much help because they were overwhelmed with their own duties.

The job in those days was utter chaos. We never really knew which boys we'd have on any given day. Success, it seemed, was getting through a shift without anyone getting hurt and with everyone fed and clothed. Activities were conducted to occupy time. Discipline was the primary method of intervention. Chores and daily living routines were troublesome necessities. We were custodians most of the time.

Treatment plans were supposed to be compiled at weekly two-hour staffings where about 20 staff members tried to talk about 36 children. This, of course, was impossible. So these meetings usually resulted in having the psychiatrist, who had seen each child for perhaps one hour in a six-month period, prescribe individual plans that most of us either never grasped or quickly forgot.

A few months after I started, the director, who had been with the agency about a year, finally convinced the board of directors to approve a team approach to working with children. We had been discussing the new concept at staff meetings and when approval finally came, everyone seemed excited.

After two or three training sessions, we were each assigned to a team, with each team having three child care workers, a social worker, and a teacher, who were responsible for six children and their families. Our new role was to design by consensus, and implement individual and family treatment plans. Psychiatrists and psychologists would be our consultants.

For many of us, this system immediately changed our attitudes about our work. We felt valued. We had more autonomy and control over what we were doing. We had a manageable group with which to work, and we were with the same children every day. We could see how the way children made their beds, the meals they ate, and the activities we chose were related to their treatment plans.

The work was still very demanding, but in a much different way. Rather than struggling through the day with little purpose other than gatekeeping, we now had to work at consensus building, support, and confrontation. I had to hold my team members accountable, and they had to do the same in relation to me. There was conflict, but it was the type of conflict that could ultimately lead to more growth.

A few persons couldn't handle the change. They were weeded out, and the director put more emphasis on hiring persons who had team skills. He instructed his supervisors to look for child care workers who had education, good communication skills, and the capacity and desire to be part of a decentralized decision-making system.

Over the next year, as a result of our trials, errors, and successes as team members, the treatment philosophy changed considerably. The notion that treatment occurred mainly in weekly visits with a therapist became passé. The new belief was that treatment took place everywhere—school, therapists' offices, the living unit, the community, in homes, and in family sessions. Solutions rested in strategies designed to teach and build strengths as well as in more traditional counseling approaches.

This shift in direction is exemplified by the following program: Three of the boys (Nick, Tim, and Willy) in our new group were several pounds overweight. We had been working at the problem by trying to get them to talk about their feelings about themselves, but they were unwilling to. They also refused to get involved in activities. It seemed the more we talked, the more resistant they became. Nick, for instance, spent more and more time lying on his bed and fantasizing that he was in the land of Oz. Tim, an arm biter, was biting and fighting more often. Willy constantly whined and complained.

The other child care workers and I were frustrated. We knew these boys felt bad about themselves and that they were subject to constant ridicule from their peers. The harder we tried to get them to talk, to get them involved in activities, the more apparent it became that we were on the wrong track. Their weight had to be the starting point, not the end result of therapy. As long as they were overweight they would feel lousy about themselves. We suggested a controlled diet, but the social worker said, "You can't deprive them of food. It's the foundation on which trust is built. If you withhold food, they won't feel nurtured, even if they are still getting more than enough to eat. The have to want to stop themselves and that won't happen until they can deal with their feelings about the past."

We respected the social worker's opinion, but we still felt there had to be another way to reach our goal. Food wasn't the only way to build trust. We could care for them in other ways. We could make sure they had an adequate amount to eat and then fill them up with special activities.

One night the three of us sat down together and began to map out a proposal to present the next day at our team meeting. It represented a drastic shift in philosophy. We contended that if we helped the boys lose weight, they would feel better about themselves. Then they would start behaving differently and be more willing to talk about their feelings.

At first the social worker resisted, but, after we explained our reasons, he decided to go along with us. He was impressed with our thoroughness and, under the new team system, committed to working toward consensus.

The program included several parts. It began in the morning with exercises—running, pushups, situps, and so on, which were followed by a weigh-in. Increases in repetitions of exercises, and decreases in weight were charted daily so that they could see their progress. At meals, we apportioned their food according to the 1,800 calorie diet prepared by the doctor and praised them for eating slowly. We also discouraged the other boys from teasing and eventually got them to support the dieters.

Three hours a week we met for "nutrition club." This time was used to discuss the nutritional value of food and to help the boys plan their own tasty low-calorie meals. These meals were then prepared with the cook once a week.

We also made a special effort to help them keep their hair combed and to make sure they took showers. We bought them special deodorants and grooming supplies. As they lost weight, we bought new clothes, had them try the clothes on, and praised them as they stood in front of the mirror.

We also involved their parents, encouraging them to help with the diets, especially when the boys were on home visits. Visits were preceded and followed with weigh-ins, and the results discussed in family sessions.

This overall approach was much more successful. There was initial resistance, of course, but as the boys lost weight they also began to feel better about themselves. They looked better and liked it. With less weight they were also able to do more exercises and participate more successfully in sports and other physical activities. The constant peer ridicule began to subside and was replaced with positive strokes. The boys gained confidence. They also began to talk about their feelings with us and in their family sessions.

This brief account of one of my early experiences in child care is representative of the change that has taken place in many residential treatment centers, group homes, and community-based programs where child and youth care workers are now an integral part of the treatment process. Contemporary workers design treatment plans with fellow team members, and then systematically weave their plans with support and care into each interaction. Their relationships with the children are still the cornerstone of effective treatment, but now they are also instrumental in determining how and where they will care for and treat their clients. In progressive organizations, team decision making, consensus building, and team supervision have replaced the old system in which clinicians, usually social workers or psychiatrists, prescribed treatments and then tried to orchestrate workers' actions from afar.

This emergence of workers into new positions of significance within the organization has also helped shift treatment from being pathology and adult-centered to being holistic and child-centered. In other words, we have brought with us positive enthusiasm and insight for understanding and helping children and their families. There is more talk now in these programs about building on strengths than about curing illnesses; more about the importance of life-space interviews [Redl 1959] than about office therapy; and more about preventive intervention than about reactive punishment. Concepts and practices such as developmental dynamics [Krueger 1983; Maier 1987; VanderVen 1979]; reeducation [Brendtro and Ness 1983]; normalization, wellness, empowerment, and self-affirmation [Beker 1986]; social skills training [Ferguson and Anglin 1985; Fox, this volume]; and total and generic teamwork [Garner 1982; Krueger 1983] that emphasize the role of a child and youth care worker, are the foundation for treatment in many organizations today.

This chapter is focused on child care organizations: residential treatment centers, group homes, and community-based programs where child and youth care workers play a major treatment role. Organizational tenets, the concepts for caring that seem to guide day-to-day interactions, are discussed first; the second part outlines an organizational process for incorporating the tenets and actions into a treatment environment. The information, which is presented as a stimulus for further discussion, is based on my experience and research in the field and my contacts with workers and supervisors in agencies across the United States and Canada. The tone and style used to describe these developments are proactive and positive. This is not to suggest that the process of developing an organization that truly cares is simple or easy, but rather to emphasize what can be done with insight and a commitment to child and youth care work.

ORGANIZATIONAL TENETS AND ACTIONS

The following tenets and corresponding actions are important in child care organizations. This list is not all-inclusive, but represents the principles and behaviors that members of these organizations seem to strive to articulate and institute on a daily basis.

Interconnected Human Systems

Child and youth care organizations are human systems whose success depends upon the ability of the people in all the systems connected with the agency—familial, community, cultural, and governmental systems—to participate in solving problems and in pursuing a set of common goals. In other words, the effectiveness of the organization is interconnected with the actions of all its members, clients, and constituents. In contemporary agencies, it is not unusual to find board members, administrators, social workers, teachers, child care workers, family members, children, and public agency social service workers all sitting down together to discuss, and work together on, solving a problem or designing a new approach to treatment. They realize that goals can be reached much more successfully through participation, compromise, and cooperation.

Caring Relationships

Caring relationships—relationships that include empathy, trust, security, compassion, and sympathy—are the foundation on which treatment is built. Managers and supervisors begin the process when they hire people who have the appropriate attributes and skills [Krueger 1986]. Then supervisors model caring interactions as they supervise and train their workers, recognizing that care for the caregivers is also a vital part of the organizational ecology [Maier 1987]. Workers, in turn, work at being caring. They are sensitive to the importance of what Maier [1979] describes as the ingredients in the core of care, the "bodily comfort, differentiations, rhythmic interactions, predictability, dependability, and personalized behavior training" that are the foundation of meaningful relationships. They also recognize that this is a highly demanding and technical task that requires self-awareness, the capacity to give and receive support from their colleagues, and the ability to communicate, model, and provide positive reinforcement [Trieschman et al. 1969].

Commitments

Caring relationships, which take time to develop and master, are nurtured by individual and organizational commitments. Perhaps the greatest hallmark of a successful program is the strength of the commitment of the workers to the organization (commitment here meaning a willingness to stay, invest energy, and grow) [Porter et al. 1974]. These commitments begin with workers' personal investments, which take into consideration that many troubled and handicapped children in placement had been psychologically and physically abandoned. Their commitments are in turn supported by organizational practices such as weekly supervision [Fleisher 1985], adequate salaries and benefits, step or promotional systems [Krueger 1986], continued education, career counseling [Fleisher 1985], and training. It is not unusual today to find some workers staying and growing for five to ten years in organizations where they receive professional and personal support.

Individualized Programming

Individual treatment plans are used to guide the development of caring relationships and the selection of intervention techniques and strategies. These plans reflect the belief that "each child or youth is viewed as a unique individual with dignity and potential who requires nurturing and encouragement" [see preface]. The child's strengths, weaknesses, and culture [Weaver, this volume], are always considered before choosing an approach. Across-the-board remedies are avoided and group treatment programs such as level systems, behavioral programs, and peer counseling are instituted only when it is clear that each individual who participates can benefit from involvement.

Wholeness, Wellness, Developmental Dynamics, and Reeducation

Troubled and handicapped children are seen as whole individuals with many strengths on which to build. The worker's task is to prevent, teach, support, and correct with strategies that are appropriate for the current levels of emotional, social, cognitive, and physical development at which a child is functioning. Reeducation, developmental, sociological, psychodynamic, psychoeducational, social learning, and ecological approaches that focus on the learning and growing that take place in daily relationships are used extensively [Brendtro and Ness 1983; Bronfenbrenner 1979; Fox, this volume; Mayer 1959; Powell, this volume; Redl and Wineman 1952].

Family and Community Involvement

Every effort is made not to treat children in isolation from their families and communities. Whether they are treated at or away from home, their families and members of their community are involved in as many facets of the treatment process as possible [Whittaker 1982; Garfat, this volume]. Workers reach out to families and try to encourage them to participate. Family members are taught parenting and social skills, counseled, and encouraged to help one another; they may also participate on treatment teams where they take part in solving problems and planning activities with staff members.

Community involvement also receives attention from the moment treatment begins until it ends. The child is encouraged and given the opportunity to spend as much time as possible with community peers and joining in activities in school, community clubs and organizations, neighborhood recreation centers, churches, and so on. Support services such as vocational training centers and youth counseling centers are also used whenever they are available and appropriate.

Purposeful Activities

Daily activities are planned in advance and evaluated afterward. Each activity, whether it is a group counseling session, dinner, bedtime, showers, a group discussion, clothes shopping, job training, money management, monopoly, or a game of kickball, is seen as having a vital role in the treatment of children and their families. In other words, activities are selected with care and insight, and planned and evaluated in relation to goals and objectives in treatment plans.

Teamwork

Treatment teams are the major mode of delivering services. Whenever possible, treatment decisions are made by consensus among team members and then carried out and evaluated together. Team members are also involved in decisions related to the administration and financing of programs, because all organizational decisions influence treatment and are enhanced by employee participation. (See below.)

Equal Status

Child and youth care workers, social workers, teachers, psychologists, and psychiatrists, are all seen as having essential roles in treatment. Further, since child and youth care workers have traditionally had less status, administrators do everything possible to provide the resources and support that will reflect their commitment to creating an environment in which child and youth care workers feel equally respected and valued [VanderVen 1979]. For example, in some organizations child care workers receive the same compensation and benefits and are given equal opportunities to advance as members of other disciplines with similar levels of education and experience [Krueger 1986].

Training and Supervision

Training and supervision are as much a part of the normal routine as other major procedures within the organization. Supervisors meet regularly with workers, using the time to teach, support, and career-counsel. Introductory and continuing inservice training, covering topics such as teamwork and communication, behavior management, daily routines, human sexuality, chemical and alcohol abuse, recreation, arts and crafts, and self-awareness, is built into everyone's working schedule. Child and youth care work is recognized as being "high tech," and like other sophisticated disciplines it requires constant review and upgrading of individual skills. One simply can't get by on experience or outdated methods of treatment.

The preceding section has offered a general description of tenets and actions that guide child-caring interactions. There are certainly others, but these are the ones that appear to be most prominent today. Its purpose has been to outline the goals that many child care organizations are striving to attain. The next step is to see how these principles and behaviors can be systematically incorporated into the organizational environment. The following is one example of how it can be done.

AN ORGANIZATIONAL PROCESS FOR CHILD AND YOUTH CARE

The process often begins when workers join other members of the organization in developing a treatment philosophy that represents their collective convictions about treatment and sets the standards from which all their actions flow. The philosophy reflects their feelings about their work and the treatment models, programs, and systems of accountability that they think are most appropriate for their setting.

A written description of the treatment philosophy is developed with input from everyone within the agency and reviewed periodically to make sure it is in tune with current beliefs, values, models, and approaches. These statements are dynamic; they change as belief and value systems and treatment technologies change.

In shaping a philosophy statement, staff members begin by discussing their attitudes about treatment. Then they proceed by choosing approaches, models, and systems of accountability that seem most consistent with their collective belief and value system. This is not a simple process. Opinions and feelings about treatment usually vary tremendously. Even within organizations where people think they share a common view of children and families, considerable hashing out of differences and compromises is usually required. Feelings about issues that affect themselves and their clients, such as abortion, chemical dependency, abuse, and human sexuality, have to be discussed in depth.

Recently, the author spent time with members of a small organization revising a two-year-old philosophy statement. It took several weekly meetings to achieve the desired outcome. The following is a sample of the results:

> Children and youths are unique and valued individuals with potential for positive change and growth. They are to be understood within the context of normal growth and development principles and viewed as whole individuals. They have a right to, and should be provided, with the following resources: shelter, clothing, food, safety, cleanliness, privacy, and health care. They also deserve to be involved in relationships that include empathy, unconditional positive regard, nurturance and support, freedom for self-expression, accessibility to adults, freedom to fail, positive expectations, and cultural and personal diversity.
>
> Treatment for each youth and his or her family is based on an individual treatment plan that is developed by our treatment team. Treatment plans are based on behavioral, ecological, reeducational, and sociological approaches. Social skills, daily living, drug counseling, recreation, arts and crafts, individual and family counseling, community living and integration, special education, physical education, and music appreciation programs are used to meet treatment goals and objectives.

> We hold ourselves accountable to this direction with standard educational and treatment tests, record keeping, written and oral daily and periodic progress tests, group and individual staff supervision, and formal annual staff evaluations.

In addition to the obvious starting place and continual reference point that a treatment philosophy provides, many helpful by-products are created during the process of writing the statement. For example, workers learn to compromise with and support one another. They can also begin to feel as if they are really a part of the organization.

With the treatment philosophy intact, members of the organization proceed to develop daily operating procedures consistent with the philosophy. Using a similar method of total involvement, they write procedures for daily operation, trying to make sure that the way the organization runs—from who changes light bulbs to what time shifts change—is first and foremost a reflection of what they consider to be in the best treatment interests of their clients.

Since operating procedures vary considerably from program to program, a set of procedures is not developed here. It is important to note, however, that effective operating procedures are almost always preceded by dynamic, as opposed to static, statements of pertinent philosophy. The vibrancy of a program, it seems, correlates directly with the relevancy of its philosophy.

The Treatment Team

Treatment teams are responsible for translating the philosophy into individual treatment plans. As they plan by consensus, team members use the statement of philosophy and the operating procedures as guides, constantly trying to choose strategies and to interact in a way that is true to their convictions about treatment.

- *Treatment Team*—A group of individuals assigned to work with specific groups of children and their families. Teams can consist of various combinations of child care workers, social workers, teachers, consultants, administrators, parents, and children. They usually average between five and eight members, but they can be as small as two or as large as ten.

- *Teamwork*—A process in which team members convene

and work together regularly to design and carry out individual treatment plans for a given number of children and their families.

- *Consensus Decision*—A decision reached through compromise and supported by all the team members.

Teams are guided into place with formal policies that promote the development of an environment in which team members can interact with one another in the most productive way possible. They provide the necessary definitions, measurable goals and objectives, clear course of action, and opportunity for equal involvement that constitute the foundation of effective teamwork. These policies include:

- Written team definitions and procedures consistent with the treatment philosophy and beliefs and values of team members [Krueger 1982].
- Goals and objectives (similar to the goals and objectives team members develop for their clients) that are regularly evaluated [Krueger 1986].
- A clear-cut decision-making process, training in teamwork and communication, and meeting schedules that accommodate everyone equally [Garner 1982; Krueger 1982].
- Procedures for minimizing departmental and/or interdisciplinary struggles [Brendtro and Ness 1983; Garner 1982; Krueger 1983; VanderVen 1979].

With the necessary structural policies in place, team members focus on teamwork. Realizing that teamwork is a sophisticated process that requires a great deal of skill, they constantly teach one another and practice team skills. The following are skills they either have or are in the process of developing:

- accepting and giving constructive feedback at team meetings and in day-to-day interactions with colleagues
- listening as fellow team members disseminate information
- advocating assertively for a specific point of view
- taking calculated risks when it is clear that a course of

action is not predetermined by a team or treatment procedure

- implementing decisions consistently
- acting independently while maintaining the trust and confidence of fellow team members
- following through dependably with team assignments and in attending meetings
- striving for and displaying self-awareness in analyzing and formulating solutions to treatment problems
- expressing anger constructively at team meetings and in individual interactions with team members
- giving and receiving support
- learning from successes and failures
- articulating observations in formal and information interactions
- writing descriptive log notes and reports
- finding a personal level of comfortableness in talking about personal issues

With a solid procedural foundation and the proper skills, team members concentrate on creating an atmosphere in which teamwork can take place. The following are human ingredients in this atmosphere:

- *Support*—Team members make a conscious effort to encourage and support one another. They set aside time to recognize particular accomplishments. They also encourage each other in their struggles to reach consensus or solve a problem.
- *Knowledge Sharing*—Team members teach each other in formal training sessions and informal interactions. They are eager to learn from one another and to share their expertise.
- *Processing*—When team members are frustrated or angry they take time to discuss and vent their feelings. They try to keep their anger and/or frustrations from undermining their efforts to work together.

- *Empathy*—Team members try to place themselves in each other's shoes, realizing that empathy is equally as important to their interactions among themselves as it is to their interactions with their clients.
- *Accountability*—Team members hold each other accountable. Through team and individual supervision they monitor each other's actions.
- *Leadership*—Team members and leaders recognize the importance of strong leadership. They respect the leader's authority and support his or her efforts to guide their interactions and decisions and his or her right to make final decisions that sometimes are in opposition to their consensus views.

Treatment Plans

A major purpose of treatment teams is developing and implementing a treatment plan for each child and his or her family. These plans, which include specific techniques, programs and/or strategies, guide day-to-day interactions.

Whenever possible, treatment plans and the techniques and strategies that make up the plans are developed by consensus. When consensus can't be reached, the team leader makes a final determination. In either case, team members try to support final decisions with equal vigor and consistency.

Treatment planning begins with the initial screening of a child and his or her family. All team members have a chance to consider the reference material and, if possible, visit or interview potential clients. If a child or family is accepted for treatment, the information gathered from this early review is used to prepare for the intake stage of treatment.

The treatment plan eventually addresses at least three stages of treatment—intake, middle, and discharge. The intake stage covers the initial adjustment to the program and, if the child is placed away from home, the initial separation from the parents or guardians and siblings. The middle stage of treatment is the period when the bulk of interacting, teaching, and relationship building takes place. The discharge stage covers the child's reintegration to a normalized condition. Although plans correspond to these stages, team members are constantly aware that planning for discharge begins on the first day. Their goal is to reintegrate as soon as possible.

The plan includes written comments and assessments from all team members, with each member focusing on his or her area of expertise. The plan also has at least four parts: a section identifying client strengths and weaknesses; a section for setting treatment objectives; a section listing techniques, strategies, and programs for meeting the objectives; and a section for evaluating progress.

Each decision about what to include or exclude from the plan is carefully weighed. Diagnostic assessments are based on the observations of all team members, which are objectively and cautiously analyzed. Decisions about what treatment techniques to include are also weighed with care and concern. Will it have a good probability of working in the current environment? Can we consistently carry it out? Is it compatible with our relationships with the child and/or family? Are they capable of meeting our expectations?

Across-the-board remedies, group programs, and standardized procedures are instituted with caution. For example, group grooming programs, positive peer groups, or privilege or level systems are instituted only when each participant's individual treatment plan indicates that this is a suitable route to take. Decisions about the color of bedspreads, the lighting in the dining room, bedtimes, tucking-ins, getting-ups, grilled cheese lunches, monopoly games, camping trips, and locations for family sessions are also individually tailored. In other words, everything possible is directed toward meeting clients' needs as identified in their treatment plans. If compromises are made because of a shortage of resources or a group management priority, they are made with a full awareness of and sensitivity to the potential drawbacks to individualized treatment.

Whenever they are using a technique or group program to eliminate or reduce a behavior or method of expression, team members are also using techniques and/or programs to teach more productive behaviors. In using a particular technique or program, they also take care not to allow them to get between themselves and the children [Trieschman 1981]. They do things with children and families and conduct their interventions with the full knowledge that their effectiveness depends directly on the quality of their relationships.

Systems of Accountability

Team members complete the process by being and holding one another accountable. They strive to be objective observers and to be articulate as they describe their observations for others. Their methods of collecting and reporting data include norm-referenced evaluations, log notes, and daily and periodic oral and written progress reports. This information is then compared to other children with similar difficulties and used to steer their movement toward their individual goals.

Progress in areas that have been identified as strengths or weaknesses is measured according to predetermined levels of acceptability. Team members are also acutely aware that they must be alert to spot progress in new or previously unidentified areas and that change can't always be measured. They use systems that help them track both designated and emerging states or conditions. Quantitative and qualitative methodologies are combined [Durkin and Durkin 1975; Krueger 1983]. Measures of behavior are always enriched with written personalized descriptions.

As they monitor progress with their clients, they also monitor their own actions. Through team and individual supervision, they challenge one another to develop skills and to learn from successes and failures. At formal evaluations, which are conducted at least twice a year, and in informal interactions, which go on constantly, they criticize and support one another, always trying to remember their basic convictions about child and youth care. As they evaluate one another, they expect no less of their interactions among themselves than they do of their interactions with the children.

SUMMARY

The tenets, actions and organizational process described here outline a direction for fruitful development of child care organizations. Movement in this direction promotes total involvement of child and youth care workers in the treatment process. It is not an easy choice to make. Resistance still exists from those who favor a more traditional or medical approach in which child and youth care workers play a less significant role, but the increasing number of agencies that are choosing and succeeding with the approach described in here offers encouragement for those who believe that this is the most effective way to care for children and their families.

REFERENCES

Beker, J. 1986. Editorial: Up from basics. *Child Care Quarterly* 15 (1):3–5.

Brendtro, L., and Ness, A. 1983. *Reeducating troubled youth: Environ-*

ments for teaching and treatment. New York: Aldine Publishing Company.

Bronfenbrenner, U. 1979. *The ecology of human development.* Cambridge, MA: Harvard University Press.

Durkin, R., and Durkin A. 1975. Evaluating residential treatment programs for disturbed children. In *The handbook of evaluative research,* ed. Struening and Gutlentag. Beverly Hills, CA: Sage Publications.

Ferguson, R., and Anglin, J. 1985. The child care profession: A vision for the future. *Child Care Quarterly* 14 (2): 85–102.

Fleischer, B. 1985. Identification of strategies to reduce turnover among child care workers. *Child Care Quarterly* 14 (2): 130–139.

Garner, H. 1982. *Teamwork in programs for children and youth.* Springfield, Il: Charles C. Thomas.

Krueger, M. 1982. Implementation of a team decision-making model among child care workers. Ph.D. diss., University of Wisconsin, Milwaukee.

Krueger, M. 1983. *Careless to caring for troubled youth.* Washington, DC: Child Welfare League of America.

———. 1986. *Job satisfaction for child and youth care workers.* Washington, DC: Child Welfare League of America.

Maier, H. 1979. The core of care: Essential ingredients for children away from home. *Child Care Quarterly* 8 (3): 161–173.

———. 1987. *Developmental group care.* New York: Hayworth Press.

Mayer, F. 1959. *A guide for child care workers.* New York: Child Welfare League of America.

Porter, L.; Steers, R.; Mawday, R.; and Boulion, P. 1974. Organizational commitment, job satisfaction and turnover among psychiatric technicians. *Journal of Applied Psychology* 59: 151–176.

Redl, F. 1959. Strategy and techniques of the life-space interview. *American Journal of Orthopsychiatry* 29: 1–18.

Redl, F., and Wineman, D. 1952. *Controls from within.* New York: Free Press.

Trieschman, A. 1981. *The anger within.* Silver Spring, MD: NAK Productions. Videotape.

Trieschman, A.: Brendtro, K.: and Whittaker, J. 1969. *The other twenty-three hours.* New York: Aldine Publishing Company.

VanderVen, K. 1979. "Towards maximum effectiveness of a unit team approach: An agenda for team development." *Residential and Community Child Care Administration* 1 (3): 287–297.

Whittaker, J. 1982. *Caring for troubled children.* San Francisco, CA: Jossey-Bass.

II

The Conflict Cycle: A Useful Model for Child and Youth Care Workers

Norman W. Powell

ERIK

When I consider the number of children and youths that I have worked with over the past 20 years, the one who had the most impact on me was Erik. Erik was six years old when he was admitted to the residential treatment center. I had been employed as a live-in child care worker for one month, my first job in the field of residential child care work. It was a small center for emotionally disturbed boys between the ages of six and 11 years. When it was explained to me that the center was a program for emotionally disturbed boys, I had no idea what that meant. Before meeting the children I tried to imagine what they would look and act like. Would they be physically deformed? Would I have to watch their every step and action? Would my life and limbs be on the line each working day?

When I finally saw the children, I was amazed at how normal they looked and behaved. I wondered why they needed to be in such a specialized mental health setting. It was not very long before I clearly understood why they required such a placement. The majority of the boys came from middle- and upper-class families who were well educated and had ample financial resources. Erik's father was a high-level official in the foreign service. The main reason for referral was that Erik's extreme acting-out behavior was disrupting the lives of his parents. The private school where he had been enrolled refused to let him remain any longer because the teachers and other staff members were not able to manage his angry outbursts or cope with the one special problem that he had—soiling. Erik would soil his pants seven or eight times every day and walk around with his smelly load. What an effective way to get negative attention and drive parents and teachers completely wild! Needless to say, when Erik arrived at our center none of the other child care workers were particularly excited about having him assigned to their group. Since I was the staff member with the least seniority, it was decided that Erik would be placed with me in my group of seven boys.

My supervisor provided me with Erik's social file and a brief oral summary of his case history. Erik began the soiling when he was four and was subject to outbursts of cursing and yelling at his parents and other adults. Many physical examinations and assessments indicated that Erik's soiling problem was emotionally based. The relationship between Erik's mother and father was reported as cold and distant. Due to his foreign service responsibilities, Erik's father had little time to be with his wife in the rearing of their son.

The day finally came for me to meet Erik. He was brought to the TV room in the residence. My first thoughts upon seeing Erik were how could such a cute, blond little boy with such deep blue eyes have so many problems and create so much trouble for the adults around him.

I said, "Hi Erik, I'm Norman, your counselor." He immediately shouted, "Fuck you, you son of a bitch!" I quickly got the sinking sensation that I was in for the challenge of my life! I felt that I had been hit with a bucket of ice water. My initial shock turned to anger. The modeling and orientation that I had received from the more seasoned workers at the center had told me that an overreaction on my part would only cause this angry boy to act out even more. I thought to myself how good it would feel to yell back at him, but I knew that yelling would only make the situation worse. This was a painful lesson that I had learned in some of my earlier encounters during the first weeks at the center.

I told Erik that I was sorry that he was so angry but when he used that language and yelled at me, it made me angry. I let him know that I was still going to be his group counselor and that I wanted to work with him, even if he did not like me or like being at the center.

Throughout the evening Erik continued to yell, scream, curse, and refuse to cooperate. My approach was to give clear oral messages and to set firm limits for him; to purposely ignore his outbursts. I was impressed with how effectively this planned ignoring seemed to work. The approach didn't make him anymore cooperative but it did minimize his yelling and cursing.

Over the following weeks Erik continued the acting out. His soiling continued at a frequency of five to six times a day. His general pattern was to carry the load in his pants until the odor became so offensive that the other children and staff members became extremely annoyed and avoided him. Whenever a staff member tried to get Erik to change his pants and wash up, he would have an angry tantrum and involve the staff member in a long and noisy power struggle.

One evening I decided to try an approach that was different from the one that the staff had been following since Erik's arrival. It was time to begin the evening routine of showers, selecting the next day's school clothes, and preparing for evening snacks. Erik threw his soiled pants on the floor next to his dirty-clothes bag. The established practice was for the child care worker to put any of his boys' soiled or dirty clothes into the washer at the end of the day.

I went over to Erik and I told him that it was now time for him to begin a new program for his soiling. I was not going to wash out his pants any longer. They were too smelly and I really didn't like doing it and felt that he should take responsibility for cleaning out his own pants. From then on, whenever he soiled his pants he was to wash them out before he could continue in any of the program activities. I took Erik to the utility sink across from the boys' bedrooms and showed him how to wash his pants with soap. He continued his cursing and resistive behavior, but he reluctantly watched my demonstration.

The following day I brought in a small scrub board and a plastic wash tub for Erik to use. After dinner, before snacks, it was obvious that Erik had loaded his pants. I brought out the scrub board and pail and reminded Erik of what we had discussed the previous evening. Erik stomped his foot, folded his arms tightly across his chest and said, "Fuck you, I'm not going to wash my damn pants."

I reminded him that he would not be able to participate in any of the evening activities until he washed out his pants and that I was prepared to stay with him until he was able to do it even if it took all night. I remarked how silly it was to take the whole evening to resist doing something that would take five minutes. After the other boys were in bed and the lights were out Erik was still refusing to wash his pants.

Shortly after 11 P.M. Erik, cursing under his breath, reluctantly picked up his pants and washed them. When he handed them to me, I saw that they were still quite soiled, and told him he had to wash them again because they were still soiled. He snatched the pants from me, called me a bastard, rewashed them, and returned with his clean pants. I thanked him and told him that he had done an excellent job. I told him to wash up and get ready for bed. I then gave him his snack, tucked him in bed and said goodnight.

Over the next several months I remained consistent and firm in my expectation that he would continue to wash his soiled pants. Although Erik still cursed and resisted at first, he always washed out his pants. Unknowingly, I had established a simple behavior modification program. Erik had always been punished by both his parents and other staff members for soiling. My focus was not on the act but on the problems created by the act—the offensive odor and general annoyance of everyone else.

When Erik's soiling decreased from seven times a day to four, I was ecstatic. It had been believed that Erik was incapable of establishing a positive relationship. Some members of the center's clinical staff did not view the decrease in soilings as anything of significance. Although they suggested that it was clinically naive to interpret this behavior as a hopeful sign, I believed that this was an important first step.

At the end of the year I made the difficult decision to accept an invitation to join the Peace Corps as a volunteer in Honduras. I knew it meant leaving the center. I gave the appropriate notice and three weeks before I was to leave I told the boys in my group. The boys expressed their sadness and several acted it out with anger. In our daily group meetings we discussed feelings about my leaving. After the second week each of the boys had worked through their feelings relatively well. Only Erik continued with his pattern of tantrums, yelling, and cursing. He refused to talk about my leaving. He repeatedly said "I am damn glad you won't be here any more. I can't wait until you leave. I'll be so happy!"

One day during my last week, Erik came up to me and to my surprise said, "Look, Norman, clean pants!" He was showing me the underpants that he had worn that day. I said that I was proud of him and that he was doing a good job with his clean pants program. For the remainder of the week he soiled only once. I also noticed that he was unusually quiet. Whenever I mentioned it, he would stomp his foot, yell several obscenities, and walk away. Finally, it was the last day. The evening program with the group went smoothly. Each boy wished me well and presented me with going-away cards that they had made with the help of the art teacher. Erik had refused to make a card.

It was bedtime, and as I said good-night and good-bye each boy wished me the best, wanted me to write and send photos. Only Erik remained quiet, with that well-known angry expression on his face. At last I came to his bed. I told him I would miss him and that I would write. He remained motionless with his arms crossed tightly against his chest. As I looked down at him to say my last good-bye, he suddenly reached up and grabbed on to me with his arms around my neck and said, "Norman, I don't want you to leave," and he began to cry very sadly. At this point the tears that had been welling up in my eyes began to roll slowly down my cheeks.

This little boy, who according to experts, was "not capable of expressing appropriate feelings and developing a positive relationship" was expressing sadness and caring.

THE CONNECTION BETWEEN SPECIAL EDUCATION AND DIRECT CARE

Child and youth care work, like many of the more established professions, has borrowed concepts from several other disciplines to enrich and expand its own body of knowledge. Medicine, social work, psychology, and education have all incorporated ideas from various other disciplines in the process of building their respective knowledge bases.

Concepts from the fields of social work, education, and psychology have been especially useful in child care work with emotionally disturbed children. The life-space interview, the therapeutic milieu, and crisis intervention are all conceptual models that have roots in other fields.

The theorists who developed these models, Fritz Redl, Bruno

Bettelheim, and Kurt Lewin, had backgrounds in the fields of education, psychoanalysis, and social psychology. As I learned subsequently in graduate training, special education also has much to contribute. Special education theories and models can be particularly beneficial in work with emotionally disturbed children.

The training I received as a direct care worker was often incidental or part of a brief orientation provided by a supervisor or coworker during the first days of employment. Much of a child care worker's training tended to be trial-and-error learning, though a few agencies provided quality ongoing training for their line workers. A recent survey of 500 child and youth care workers found that the average inservice training time provided by their agencies was only 42.3 hours per year [Krueger et al. 1987]. Most child care training in the U.S. is primarily experiential, often unstructured, unsystematic, and lacking in relevant conceptual models. As a result, many workers in the field have developed competence in their daily work with children but are unable to adequately articulate what they do in universally recognized clinical language.

As a line worker I learned how to develop a daily program for a group of disturbed children. I also developed skills in crisis intervention and in relationship building. However, it was still not until I entered the special education graduate program in emotional disturbance that I was able to make an important connection between my line experience and the academic training. The didactic presentation of conceptual course content, combined with daily supervised classroom teaching, provided a structured learning experience unique to the field of education. Every task had to be approached sequentially, daily lesson plans had to be developed, and individual educational objectives were clearly defined. A structure and discipline were required that had not been expected of me in my work with children. For the first time, I was able to understand the relationship between my work experience and the principles upon which the therapeutic goals of that experience were based. I was then able to adopt conceptual frameworks that offered me a deeper understanding of children's behavior and emotional disturbance, and a guide to working with disturbed children.

THE MODEL AND SOME BACKGROUND

The Conflict Cycle Model was the most important theory I learned. It was several years after the experience with Erik that this model helped me to understand the complicated power struggle in which the boy and I had been involved.

This model was developed by a noted special educator, Dr. Nicholas J. Long, and was based on psychodynamic theory [Long 1966; Brendtro and Ness 1983; Morse 1985; Powell 1983]. Long used this model to train teachers to understand the dynamics of power struggles in their work with disturbed children.

Long began as an elementary school educator and received his doctorate in educational psychology. While a graduate student, he developed an interest in emotional disturbance as a child care worker at the University of Michigan's Fresh Air Camp for disturbed children. It was here that he met the renowned child care specialist, Fritz Redl. Redl was a consultant for the camp and served as an important model for Long. Redl and his colleague, David Wineman, along with other noted consultants at the camp, demonstrated for Long the principles that change in destructive behavior "evolves and revolves around relationships" and "all behavior has meaning and the meaning is frequently symbolic and or self-protective" [Kauffman and Lewis 1974].

Long held a number of distinguished positions directing special education and mental health programs and projects for disturbed children. He and Redl directed a well-known residential research study of aggressive behavior in adolescents. During his tenure as director of Hillcrest Children's Center in Washington, D.C., Long began to expand on his Conflict Cycle Model, drawing on ideas that evolved from his earlier work experiences.

One important assumption of this model is that the quality of the early life experiences of children can significantly affect their personality development. If vital developmental growth needs are not adequately met during these formative years, it is probable that children will have much social and emotional difficulty. It is during this early period that children's self-concept, worldview, and values begin to develop.

The way in which children perceive themselves and the world will often influence their behavior and response to stress. If this worldview is distorted and generally negative, their reaction to daily stresses and demands will be negative and ineffective [Long et al. 1986]. Children who are so lacking in social and emotional competence are considered to be disturbed, or what Morse [1985] refers to as "socioemotionally impaired." When confronted with a stressful situation their response is often negative and tends to provoke counteraggression and negative reactions from others. To enable professionals to better understand the application of his model, Long established several operating principles. The following summarizes the important points of these principles:

- Children in conflict view the situation and the world in terms of their life history.
- Children in stress will create their feelings and often their behaviors in adults.
- Crises are opportune times for adults to model and teach social and emotional competence.
- For children under stress we must reinterpret adult intervention as an act of support and protection rather than hostility.
- We must view children in terms of their strengths and weaknesses and avoid diagnostic stereotypes.
- Raising the self-esteem of children promotes social, emotional, and intellectual growth.
- We must develop the ability to acknowledge and accept the feelings of children without necessarily accepting the way in which they choose to express them.

These principles were based on the "psychoeducational model" of special education. Long has been a major proponent of this approach [Kauffman and Lewis 1974]. The model provides a means of analyzing and understanding the elements of power struggles that we have with children in stress, describing how the interaction during a confrontation between an adult and a child follows a circular pattern. This conflict or confrontation typically starts as the result of a stressful incident that occurs in the classroom, the residential center, or some other area within the child's life space.

The adult may or may not have been involved in the initial incident, where it is usually the result of the child's irrational overreaction to some type of physical, psychological, developmental, and/or reality stress that he or she is experiencing [Fagan et al. 1986]. During this process the attitudes, feelings, and behaviors of the child are influenced by the attitudes, feelings, and reactions of the adult involved. Likewise, the attitudes, feelings, and behaviors of the adult are influenced by the child's reactions and attitudes.

This negative cycle of interaction is difficult for the adult to interrupt constructively. There is an automatic urge on the part of the adult to overreact to the child's negative behavior and to respond defensively. When the adult does overreact, a destructive power struggle develops in which winning becomes the primary objective for both adult and child [Long et al. 1986]. This model enables us to focus not only on the feelings and behavior of the child but also on those of the adult. A basic tenet of the model is that conflicts and power struggles are perpetuated when an adult responds impulsively to the child's negative behavior.

Over the past 15 years I have used this model to train hundreds of child care workers and teachers in a variety of settings throughout North America. On several occasions it was also used to train hearing-impaired teachers and child care workers. The responses from all these groups were equally receptive and enthusiastic, demonstrating the model's wide applicability.

The following is a description of the components of the Conflict Cycle Model. This description is based primarily on Long's psychoeducational concept, with modifications that I made to adapt the model to child and youth care work. In this adapted version there are three preconditioning components: self-concept, worldview, and values. There are four primary components: the stressful incident, the feelings, the observable behavior, and the response. The three preconditioning components are the result of the children's early life experiences. They greatly influence the four primary components and how children express themselves during each of these component stages of the conflict cycle.

The Self-Concept

The self-concept is a representation of children's perception of themselves in relation to their early life experiences and environment [Rogers 1965]. Children respond to stress and other environmental demands in ways that are consistent with this self-concept. Much of the self-concept is based on the quality of the responses that children receive from significant others in their environment [Coopersmith 1967]. If this feedback has been consistently negative and nonsupportive, children's concepts of themselves and their reactions to others similarly will be affected. For example, children who have received much rejection in their early life from parents, peers, and others become susceptible to developing a negative self-image, hostility toward others, and a lack of social and emotional competence [Garbarino 1982; Morse 1985].

The Worldview

The second preconditioning component is the worldview, which consists of children's perception of the world, how it operates, what the rules are, and what one must do to meet needs and achieve goals. Like the first component, the worldview is primarily a product of the quality and kind of experiences that children had during their early formative years. If their experience demonstrated that adults are hostile, abusive, and untrustworthy, they will likely have this perception of people and the world in general. Children's perceptions of the world represent reality for them no matter how distorted or limited their perspective might be [Rogers 1965]. The behavior of others will be interpreted by children in accordance with their particular view of the world.

Disturbed children develop a self-fulfilling prophecy based on their view of the world. It is the child's cognitive effort to understand and rationalize the neglect, pain, and abuse received earlier in life. For example, for children who believe that adults are physically and emotionally abusive, it makes sense not to trust them and to reject their friendly overtures. The self-fulfilling prophecy provides these children with justifications for their negative attitudes and behavior toward adults. When the children are successful at engaging adults and peers in destructive conflicts and power struggles, their view of a hostile world is reinforced and the prophecy becomes fulfilled [Long et al. 1986]. Disturbed children have learned to be extremely skillful at involving adults and peers in these destructive confrontations. Efforts on the part of caring adults to help and support the children are continually rejected because these gestures threaten their ability to fulfill their established prophecy. An aggressive disturbed child will devote much energy to provoking counteraggression from others. When the behavior of the people in the child's environment is consistent with the child's worldview, the child feels secure because the environment remains predictable, familiar, and manageable, even though this security is based on a bizarre and counterproductive model.

Values

The third component is comprised of children's values, the internalized principles, rules of behavior, and beliefs that they have acquired from their early environment. These values have been modeled by the significant adults and others in the children's environment [Bandura 1973]. The quality of the value system is primarily a product of the quality of the values to which children have been exposed. Values are also a reflection of the children's socioeconomic and cultural experience [Rogers 1965]. Children raised in an environment in which daily survival depends on one's ability to fight place a different value on physical aggression than children from an environment where this need is nonexistent.

The values of those involved play an important role in the perpetuation of a power struggle. Adults often overreact to behaviors and attitudes of children that are expressions of value systems that conflict with the value systems of the adults. For example, I recall a situation in which an inexperienced child care worker became involved in a physical confrontation with one of his group home residents because the boy refused to remove his cap upon entering the house. The boy had come from an environment in which his peers wore their caps because it was the current fad and their machismo system. The worker's body language and tone of voice communicated such hostility that the boy reacted angrily. He refused to remove his cap and began to curse and yell. The worker tried to remove the cap, but the boy resisted and the worker began to struggle with him. Hearing the uproar, several other staff members intervened and pulled the worker and boy apart.

Central to this conflict was the worker's extreme reaction to the wearing of the cap. The worker had been raised to believe that wearing a cap inside was unacceptable. More stress was created for him when the boy began to curse and yell at him. These angry expressions of behavior were also unacceptable according to the worker's personal values.

It is certainly appropriate to establish a set of value expectations for children or youths in residence to follow. Efforts to get them to concur with these established expectations should be made with skill and sensitivity, and with the recognition that their value systems will often clash with our own. In our work with children we must develop the ability to handle the stress that is created when we are confronted with conflicting value systems so that we, in turn, can respond constructively to negative behavior.

Stress

The first primary component of the Conflict Cycle is stress.

Stress, or more specifically, the stressful incident, can be referred to as the first phase of the cycle. In "The Pointer," Long defines stress as "a subjective reaction to external conditions that are real, anticipated, or imagined and that cause physiological and/or psychological discomfort" [Long et al. 1986]. He identifies four types of stress: physical stress; psychological stress; reality stress or unplanned events; and developmental stress.

In our daily lives a number of factors cause us to experience stress, which can motivate us toward positive activity or overwhelm us and cause panic, flight, or attack [Sawrey and Telford 1968]. The manner in which one responds to stress depends on a combination of factors. Among these are the degree of stress experienced, the nature of the stress, and our individual physical, psychological, and emotional makeup [Lewis 1971].

According to the Conflict Cycle Model, our socialization history combines with our worldview, our self-concept, and our values, to greatly influence our responses to daily stress. Each of these components of our experience and personality plays a role in affecting how we perceive a stress-creating situation or event. In the example above, the negative manner in which the worker responded caused the stress for the youngster. As a result, he responded negatively, and this in turn caused more stress for the worker.

Though many factors can contribute to a person's feeling of stress in a given situation, it is the stressful incident that precipitates the negative cycle behavior. The stressful incident for the worker in the example above occurred when the youngster entered the group home wearing a cap. For the youngster, the stressful incident occurred when the worker angrily demanded that the youngster remove his cap. Stress was created for each of these individuals and both responded negatively and became involved in a destructive power struggle.

Feelings

Feelings are our inherent responses to environmental stimuli and events. The Austrian psychiatrist, Alfred Adler, referred to feelings as innate "response potentials" [Ford and Urban 1963]. In the Conflict Cycle Model it is the stress caused by the stressful incident that feeds the second phase of the cycle, the feelings. Many feelings can be generated by the stressful incident—anger, fear, helplessness, frustration, counter aggression, anxiety, and so on. We have all experienced the world differently, and therefore the feelings caused by stressful situations will vary according to our experiences and individual perceptions.

Behavior

The feelings phase of the Conflict Cycle feeds and influences behavior, which is the next phase in the model. The behavior phase represents the observable expression of the feelings of the individuals involved in the conflict situation. "Whenever we act in a certain way, we act not in accordance with the reality of the situation as it confronts us, but according to our subjective appraisal of it" [Dreikurs and Grey 1968].

According to Adler's followers, behavior is the result of our subjective interpretation of life situations. We draw on our past experiences to make judgments about the present. Much of our ability to evaluate and interpret the realities of day-to-day living is based on how well we have interpreted the events of our early childhood.

As humans we all express our feelings through some form of behavior. Our ability to express feelings in appropriate and constructive ways is related primarily to the early modeling and socialization to which we were exposed. For disturbed and troubled children this early modeling and socialization was not sufficiently constructive, and their response to daily demands, stresses, and problems has consistently manifested itself in negative and counterproductive behavior. This behavior represents their most immediate effort to cope with a situation or incident that is creating stressful feelings.

Response

The behavior phase of the cycle pushes the conflict to the next phase—response. The Conflict Cycle is an interactive model. In the typical conflict situation a power struggle is occurring between a child and a child care worker. The child reacts to some stressful incident, becomes very angry, and begins to kick the trash can in the group home dining room. The worker intervenes and gives a clear verbal message to the youngster that this destructive behavior is unacceptable and is to be stopped. A key principle of the model is that the *quality* of a child care worker's response to a child's negative behavior can affect the child's stress level. If the worker overreacts to the negative behavior, the child's stress will increase.

In the intensity of a power struggle between a worker and a child, the goal of the worker's response should be to minimize the child's level of stress. If the child's stress can be decreased, the child's feelings and behavior will become less overt, and the child will become more available for the worker's attempts to resolve the conflict constructively.

The responsibility for ending the negative cycle of this power struggle is the worker's. It is assumed that the worker has the maturity, understanding, and the experience to respond to a crisis situation in a constructive and professional manner. The ability to respond constructively to stress and the negative behavior of children is an essential competency in child care work. The quality of a worker's response in a stress-filled power struggle can provide a child with a constructive model for developing the social and emotional competence that he or she is lacking.

In considering the four primary components of the Conflict Cycle, it is the response phase that provides the worker with the greatest opportunity to model for the child.

A CONFLICT CYCLE EXAMPLE

It is dinner time at the residential treatment center. The cafeteria is filled with the noise of children and staff members involved in completing the evening meal.

Mark, a new resident, walks back to his table with his tray of food. As he begins to sit down, Bobby, the boy seated in the chair next to him accidently knocks over Mark's cup of milk. It spills on the table and runs down into Mark's chair. Mark calls Bobby "a dumb ass!" Bobby jumps up and shouts obscenities back and pushes Mark. At this moment a new child care worker, Howard, runs over and grabs Mark from behind. When the worker grabs Mark, the boy begins to struggle and curse at the worker, who yells at Mark and tells the boy to stop using "foul language" and to calm down. The boy resists the worker's efforts to hold him. Howard holds the boy tighter.

By now the cafeteria is in an uproar, and the other child care workers try to calm the groups of children seated at the other tables. The struggle becomes more physical. The worker and boy end up rolling around on the floor. Other staff members intervene and finally Mark is removed from the room. This is a typical example of what can happen when a child care worker overreacts to a conflict cycle situation.

The Boy

In analyzing this example, let us look first at the boy, Mark. We have little information about his social history except that he is 15 years old, comes from a broken home, and was removed from five foster homes before his admission to the residential center; he has been at the center for two weeks.

Worldview

The boy probably sees the world as a dangerous place in which everyone will try to take advantage of him. It is therefore necessary to protect himself. He probably has little trust in adults. He possibly feels that the world has treated him unjustly, and one way to get respect and maintain control is to have the ability to defend oneself.

Self-concept

That the boy is a product of a broken home and had been removed from several foster homes indicates that his sense of self-worth is probably very low.

Values

This youngster has had to learn to protect himself from peers and adults. His response to verbal and physical attack has been to fight back.

Stress

In considering this youngster's overall situation, one can easily understand that the boy has had much stress in his life and that his ability to manage daily stress would not be very good. The stressful incident in the example occurred when Bobby knocked over Mark's milk. More stress was created when the child care worker grabbed Mark from behind.

Feelings

The boy must have experienced a number of feelings in this situation: anger—at the other boy and at the child care worker; frustration—he didn't initiate the problem; embarrassment—being singled out in front of his peers; helplessness—he didn't create the situation but he still was grabbed by the worker; vulnerability—there was seemingly no one there to defend him. When the worker intervened he didn't say anything to the other boy, Bobby, who caused the milk to spill and who pushed Mark. This must have made Mark feel that he had been unjustly treated by the worker.

Behavior

The boy expressed his feelings of stress in a number of ways. He cursed at the other boy and he was defiant toward the child care worker. (See figure 1.)

Worker's Response

The worker overreacted and responded negatively to the crisis and contributed to the perpetuation of the conflict situation instead of responding in a way that would have caused less stress for himself and the boy. When we look at what has created the stress, feelings, and behavior for the boy, it is important that we try to understand how the youngster has interpreted or perceived the worker's response to his behavior.

In this example, the youngster probably perceived that the child care worker was trying to hurt him and was going to treat him unjustly. Therefore, the intervention of the worker created greater stress, more overt feelings and more negative behavior.

This model is different from other models because not only does it help us to analyze the stress, feelings, and behavior of the child it also allows us to analyze the stress, feelings, and behavior of the child care worker involved.

The Child Care Worker

In looking at the worker's role in the conflict situation, the only information that we have is that he is a new child care worker. Regarding his worldview, self-concept, and values we can make several observations.

Worldview

He probably believes that children should be respectful of adults and that as an adult authority figure he has a responsibility to maintain order and control.

Self-Concept

As a new child care worker, he most likely has some insecurity about his role and his abilities in this new job situation.

Values

He believes that physical force is an effective way to respond to crisis situations with children. He also believes that it is inappropriate for youngsters to use obscene language.

Figure 1.
The Conflict Cycle Model
Child ⟶ Worker

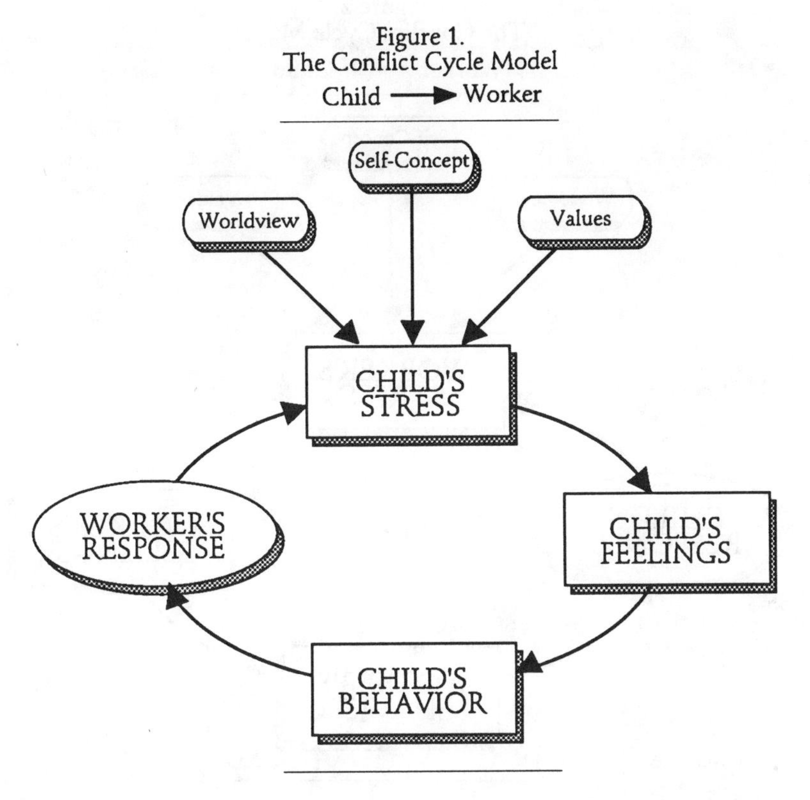

Stress

In this situation several things caused the worker's stress. He was new to the job and the crisis at dinner probably made him anxious. It was also important for him to be able to demonstrate to his supervisors that he was able to manage the crisis. The stressful incident for the worker took place when Mark called Bobby a name and the boy pushed Mark. Greater stress was caused when Mark began to resist and struggle with him, the worker.

Feelings

The worker probably experienced the following: anger—because the youngster was resisting physically; fear—that the situation would get more out of control; aggression—the boy was angry and aggressive so it was necessary to meet this behavior with equal aggression; insecurity—about his ability as a new worker to handle this crisis situation.

Figure 2.
The Conflict Cycle Model
Worker ⟶ Child

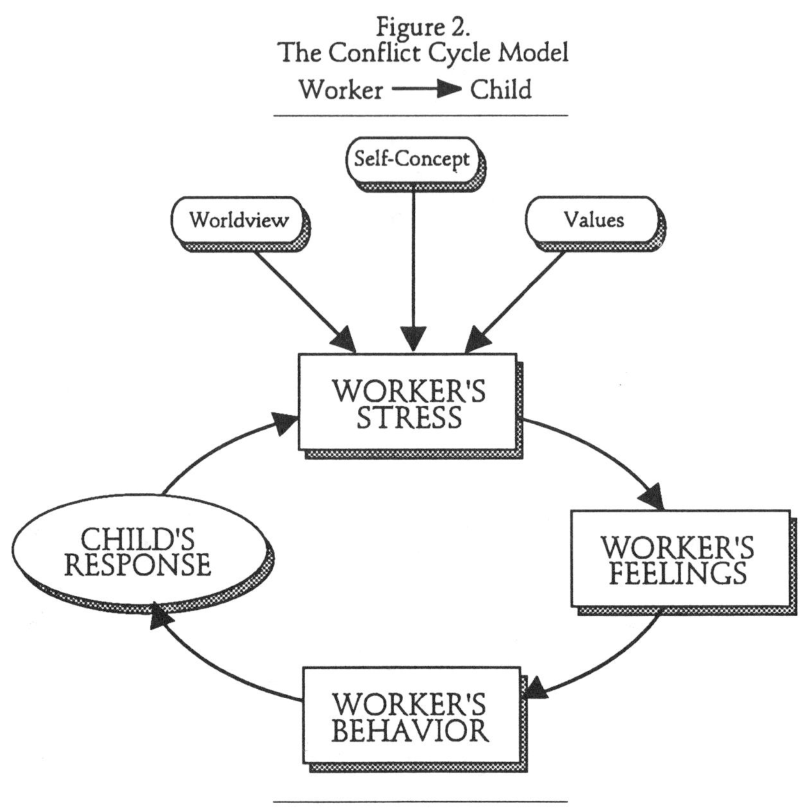

Behavior

The worker expressed his feelings by yelling and using physical force.

Child's Response

The worker perceived the child's response as defiant and aggressive. This response from the child created greater stress and more overt feelings and behavior on the part of the worker. The child's stress, feelings, and behavior were duplicated by the child care worker. (See figure 2.)

SUMMARY

Here we have applied the model in analyzing an example of a negative power struggle between a child care worker and a child. The worker was inexperienced and became negatively involved in the struggle for power and control with the child. Experienced and well-trained workers would not have let the stress and intensity of the situation overwhelm them. They would have known not to use physical force and would have intervened in a more supportive and less stress-producing manner. They would have quickly been able to move the two boys to some other area where they could talk about the incident in a less tension-filled environment. They would also have known how to use their body language and voice quality to minimize the stress for both of the boys.

This model can be used to train staff members and children to better understand daily conflicts and ways to avoid destructive conflict situations. It can also be used to help parents better understand the power struggles that they get into with their children. It has been developed by special educators and has been useful in working with children and youths in residential and group care settings.

REFERENCES

Bandura, A. 1973. *Aggression: A social learning analysis.* Englewood Cliffs, NJ: Prentice Hall.

Brendtro, L., and Ness, A. 1983. *Re-educating troubled youth: Environments for teaching and treatment.* New York: Aldine Publishing Company.

Coopersmith, S. 1967. *The antecedents of self-esteem.* San Francisco, CA: Freeman.

Dreikurs, R., and Grey, L. 1968. *A new approach to discipline: Logical consequences.* New York: Hawthorne Books, Inc., 23.

Ford, D., and Urban, H. 1963. *Systems of psychotherapy.* New York: John Wiley and Sons, Inc., 317.

Gabarino, J. 1982. *Children and families in the social environment.* New York: Aldine Publishing Company, 38.

Kauffman, J. M., and Lewis, C. D. 1974. *Teaching children with behavior disorders.* Columbus, OH: Charles E. Merrill, Co., 173.

Krueger, M.; Lauerman, R.; Beker, J.; Savicki, V.; Parry, P.; and Powell, N. 1987. Professional child and youth care work in the United States and Canada: a report of the NOCCWA Research and Study Committee. *Journal of Child and Youth Care Work* 3: 17–31.

Lewis, M. 1971. *Clinical aspects of child development: An introductory synthesis of psychological concepts and clinical problems.* Philadelphia, PA: Lea and Febiger, 33-35.

Long, N. 1966. Direct help to the classroom teacher: a consultant role for the school psychologist. *School Research Program.* Washington, D C.: The Washington School of Psychiatry.

Long, N.; Fagen, S.; and MacArthur, C. 1986. *The Pointer* 30 (3): 9–11.

Long N.; Morse, W.; and Newman, R. (1976). *Conflict in the classroom* . 3rd ed. Belmont, CA: Wadsworth Publishing Company, 238.

Morse, W. C. 1985. *The education and treatment of socio-emotionally impaired children and youth.* Syracuse, NY: Syracuse University Press, 80.

Powell, N. 1983. *The use of the Conflict Cycle Model and the twelve techniques for the classroom management of surface behavior by residential child care workers to increase competence in the behavior management of aggressive children.* Washington, DC: The American University.

Rogers, C.R. 1965. *Client-centered therapy.* Boston, MA: Houghton Mifflin Company, 484–485, 497–498.

Sawrey, J., and Telford, W. C. 1968. *Psychology of adjustment.* 2d ed. Boston, MA: Allyn and Bacon, Inc., 412.

III

Social Skills Training: Teaching Troubled Youths to be Socially Competent

Richard G. Fox

SCOTT

I first met Scott in an intake interview before his placement in a residential treatment center for disturbed and delinquent youths. He was a bright, attractive youngster but full of anger, depression, and denial. He was being placed because he had stolen an automobile with a group of adolescent boys. This had followed on the heels of a number of burglaries, all of which were committed under the influence of alcohol and drugs. Reports indicated that Scott's behavior vacillated from an uncommunicative, depressive state to active levels of chemical use, delinquency, and impulsiveness. And, indeed, in the interview he refused to acknowledge responsibility for his actions and minimized the feelings that he was experiencing about his placement, family struggles, and chemical addiction.

After placement, we learned that Scott's family history was not especially remarkable compared to other youngsters in residential treatment. His mother had remarried after a failed 12-year marriage to Scott's father. Scott reported that his formative years were characterized by much turmoil and conflict due to his father's chemical dependency, unemployment, and domestic violence. Scott's stepfather, however, was beginning to provide a stabilizing influence in this previously dysfunctional family. Although Scott's mother was largely incapable of managing the family by herself before and after the divorce, she was beginning to acquire a sense of direction and confidence about parenting following the remarriage, especially with Scott's younger brother and sister.

From Scott's perspective, however, the damage had been done when his mother's first marriage failed and he experienced the brunt of his father's alcoholism and violent tendencies. He said that he had probably experimented with drugs in junior high as much to enhance his relationships in his delinquent peer group as to provide escape from his family situation, and the accompanying depression and hopelessness evolving from it. Though reasonably bright, his academic achievement had suffered, especially in the transition from elementary school to junior high, with periods of truancy and school misconduct occurring as he moved into high school. At the time of placement, he had been expelled from school as a result of a drug-buying incident.

It was clear from an analysis of the information gained during the preplacement interviews with Scott and his parents and from psychological reports and case history that Scott needed a program of intervention directed at least in part to the acquisition of social skills, especially in regard to expressing feelings, establishing and maintaining relationships with peers, resisting peer pressure, and making decisions. Furthermore, he needed to apply these skills in not only a social context but also within the family setting.

The primary goal of human services is to develop a course of treatment and intervention for troubled youngsters and their families that will make them socially competent in the broadest sense. Scott and his family as described in the vignette are an example of a human system in distress and clearly lacking in the resources and competence to respond to the crisis in which they were enmeshed. Scott was deficient in the necessary skills to deal with stress, peer pressure, the expression of feelings, and decision making related to the use of chemicals. His mother was struggling with her own dilemmas and was powerless to provide models for him to handle the problems he was experiencing and to resolve the conflict that she, also, was personally experiencing.

Children and youths in conflict are, generally speaking, individuals having difficulties in social competence. Their inability to negotiate successfully the demands of the social environment causes untold grief and pain in their lives and the lives of the families from which these youngsters come. Often the problems can be directly related to the absence of specific social and personal skills. Underachievement, chemical abuse, delinquency, and other conditions that characterize this population of children often rest on weak or limited social skill repertoires. Scott is a tragic example of this analysis. Granted that he never had the opportunity to acquire some of these skills or to be exposed to effective models. Yet it is almost self-evident to predict that more viable skills in stress reduction, expression of feelings, and decision making might have helped him respond more effectively to the problems to which he was exposed.

Children and youths, like Scott, placed in group care facilities for treatment of physical, emotional, cognitive, and behavioral problems are often viewed and understood from a variety of terms and constructs. For example, they might be described according to handicapping conditions, pathological states, socioeconomic status, and/or juvenile justice dispositions. Originally intended to give human service professionals including child and youth care workers a more thorough picture of the problems of these youths, it seems that this labeling process has left many workers struggling with initiating a treatment plan and identifying a central, unifying principle around which these diverse youths can be best understood.

It does not seem surprising, therefore, that child and youth care, with its emphasis on developing social, educational, and caring relationships [Trieschman et al. 1969; Brendtro and Ness 1983; Maier 1979] in the total life space of the youngster, has turned to social competence, a conceptualization within which all children can be understood [White 1978]. In mapping out their visions for the future of the child care profession, Ferguson and Anglin [1985] claim that "child care has developed within a model of social competence rather than in a pathology-based orientation to child development." Fox and Krueger [1986] have asserted:

> Yet, while the field seems to have naturally moved toward this unifying body of theory, it has only begun to explore and articulate its applications to practice. For example, a review of current literature in child and youth care produces few examples of how social competence theory can be used in the milieu and only cursory references to the work of leaders in this area.

In this chapter, therefore, the author describes the basic concept of social competence and social skills training procedures that will help lead to social competence for youngsters served in group care facilities.

Social competence theory proposes that all individuals possess a collection of behaviors that are more or less adaptive and influence their ability to conform to the expectations and standards established by society [White 1959]. The more competent the individuals are in the social domain (as well as in the other developmental domains), the more likely they are able to respond appropriately to the requirements of their culture. Conversely, the less competent they are, the less likely they are able to respond adaptively.

Typically, upon admission to a treatment center, an assessment process to study the characteristics of youngster and family is set into operation. Assessment may involve looking at the family, social, educational, community, and self systems through which these youngsters pass. The goal is to identify the reasons for the failure of children and families to develop and function adaptively. Some would contend, however, that all too often this activity focuses mainly on identifying and alleviating the pathological conditions that have brought about the need for treatment rather than describing repertoires that need to be acquired, strengthened, or changed. Further, it is important to recognize that this may well be the very failing of this assessment process, since the emphasis on isolating and identifying negative behaviors may not always be accompanied by an attempt to identify positive behaviors that should be developed and refined. It is not difficult, then, to understand why the treatment may focus on the alleviation of "sickness." Nonetheless, whether the problem be with the assessment process or the attitudes of the practitioner, the end results often leave human services workers looking for something positive to do.

Theorists and practitioners associated with the evolving body of practice and research on social skills training suggest that these youngsters end up in treatment programs because they are manifesting limited and antisocial behavioral repertoires. In other words, they are socially incompetent or dysfunctional, as are their families, and without direct training and intervention to build more positive behaviors little will occur to directly enhance these youngsters' abilities to deal effectively with the personal and social demands of their environment. It also needs to be recognized that it is because of deficiencies in this domain that youngsters are not able to benefit from other programmatic interventions like education, vocational training, and independent-living opportunities. Social skills training represents a step in the direction of responding to these needs.

THEORETICAL ORIGINS AND SOCIAL COMPETENCE

Social skills training methods represent a melding of techniques, many of which were derived from social learning theory literature. Behavioral outcomes evolved from the extension of social competence theory and vocational adjustment research on adult handicapped. It can be described as a structured and direct teaching approach that facilitates the acquisition, production, and generalization of personal and social behavior. For the purposes of this discussion, personal behavior is defined as that which is directed to oneself and can be characterized as intra-individual in nature. In most cases, depending on the theorist, this refers to such broad functions as feelings, self-esteem, stress reduction, and so on. In a practical sense, this may be operationalized as teaching the youngsters to label their feelings, display self-control, deal with failure, and so forth.

Social behavior, however, is defined as that which is directed to others and can be characterized as inter-individual exchanges. Here the reference is to interpersonal behavior, aggression management, expression of affect, and so forth. This may mean such behaviors as cooperation, sharing feelings, apologizing, sportsmanship, and other behaviors depending on the population, setting, and program.

One might ask how individuals acquire personal and social competence. What systems are operating to ensure that people behave according to some minimal level of decorum? Although society often does not approach this issue directly or systematically, a number of behavioral acquisition and intervention systems overlap and operate in homes, schools, and communities, and respond to the deficiencies in the personal and social skill repertoires of children and youths. Although these systems may not share similar mandates, espouse compatible philosophies, or respond to the same constituencies, they may provide societal and structural responses to the social development needs of children and youths, especially those in conflict or crisis.

These systems include discipline systems, special interventions, prosthetic environments, and incidental learning. Proponents of social skills training would suggest that the one system that is lacking or often unrecognized is the direct instruction of personal-social competence. (See table 1.)

Discipline systems, which this author refers to as the traffic cop model, operate in many environments and emphasize the delivery of punitive consequences for the occurrence of inappropriate behaviors. Although this approach may be immediately effective, its effects may not endure over time, it may evoke troublesome emotional responses, and it may not generalize to a broader range of settings. For example, public school environments are notorious for employing discipline systems of one sort or another. Their goal is to prevent and control negative behavior through the application of punitive consequences. More to the point, however, is the absence of any instruction that will allow the individual to avoid the negative consequences that characterize this system. It is not uncommon in discipline systems for youngsters to be left on their own to determine what is appropriate and inappropriate behavior.

Some child care programs operate in this same manner by establishing levels of consequences and behavioral expectations sometimes referred to as level or step systems. Although practitioners may take great care to point out the expectations in these settings in preplacement reviews or orientations, the emphasis still is on the application of consequences without accompanying attention to the teaching of acceptable behavior. To return to the metaphor of driving and traffic cops, we are rarely reinforced by the legal authorities for driving carefully and we are not taught by those agencies to any significant degree to drive safely. When we make an error or drive carelessly, however, the likely response of this system is punitive.

Special interventions—the magic bullet model—are often a response to the ineffectiveness of discipline systems over the long haul. Special interventions are those responses of the treatment community to the acute personal and social needs of an individual or groups often delivered in an atmosphere of heightened expectations regarding outcome. For example, after a number of suicides have occurred in a school, authorities may allocate money for experts to consult with and train teachers, to purchase new and exciting curricula and educational materials on suicide and depression in children, and to establish special support groups and classes

TABLE 1

Approaches for Achieving Social Competence

	SYSTEM	FOCUS	ADVANTAGES	LIMITATIONS
DISCIPLINE SYSTEMS	Traffic cop	Application of consequences	Immediate effect	Short-lived Reactive No teaching
SPECIAL INTER-VENTIONS	Magic bullet	Special treat-ment with heightened ex-pectations	Halo effect Short-term effectiveness	Short-lived Reactive No teaching
PROSTHETIC ENVIRON-MENTS	Health spa	Protected settings	Frees treat-ment from distractions	Problems in generali-zation Reactive
INCIDENTAL LEARNING	Monkey-see, monkey-do	Learning by observation	Automatic	All children do not benefit Nonsystematic
DIRECT INSTRUCTION	Three R's	Systematic teaching	Proactive	Violates ex-pectations of accepted practice Absence of resources

for high-risk children. Another example is the use of insight-building techniques such as psychotherapy to cognitively restructure children's understanding of the events that they have been experiencing relative to their problems.

Unfortunately, these ways of responding to the personal and social needs of children are reactive: the problem has to occur before society concerns itself with it. In addition, as with discipline systems, the effects of special interventions are often short-lived, especially if there are no enduring changes in the environment to prevent the problem from recurring. For example, have there been preventive efforts to develop in children the discrete skills for dealing with stress, isolation, and depression, and for softening the impact of dysfunctional family systems—the factors associated with suicide?

Prosthetic environments—the health spa model—have always been used in the treatment of troubled or limited individuals. This model purports that the behavioral demands of the individual are so great that he or she cannot be treated efficiently in the real-life setting and requires the support of a specialized and, often, artificial environment for a period of time. It should be noted that isolation from the natural setting is a characteristic of this model, and that special discipline systems and special interventions are often employed in these specialized environments. Residential treatment centers, drug rehabilitation hospitals, and special education programs are examples of prosthetic environments.

Of course there are problems that limit the effectiveness of this approach. One is the matter of generalization. It is not an uncommon occurrence for significant behavior changes to be noted in the treatment setting only to be followed by relapse or behavior degeneration after reintegrating the individual into the natural setting. However, these environments are quite effective in producing social competence for a period of time if no longer than the period of isolation from the real-life setting.

The larger share of behavioral acquisition is produced by incidental learning. Children imitate the behavior to which they are constantly exposed. This monkey-see, monkey-do model operates around the clock, in the presence of both positive and negative models, and is largely automatic. Unfortunately, it is not without its limitations. For example, some children are not exposed to the best models, so they have strong and competing responses for the appropriate social behaviors that we would like them to acquire. Also, some children do not always have the best conditions under which to learn appropriate social behavior; their homes are chaotic, families dysfunctional, and/or learning mechanisms flawed.

Advocates of social skills training suggest that while the foregoing models are necessary and reasonably effective in developing socially competent individuals, they are not sufficient by themselves or in isolation, especially for troubled and handicapped youths. In response, they propose that the 3 R's model or the direct instruction of personal and social skills be employed to increase the probability that these youngsters will attain socially competent behavior. It should be noted that this model is proactive in contrast to the reactive nature of the other models. It proposes what skills youngsters should learn and sets about teaching them rather than deciding after the fact what should be taught. Furthermore, practitioners within this model insist that this process of instruction be systematic, occur on a regular basis, and be delivered in the natural setting as well as the treatment environment.

SOCIAL SKILLS TRAINING AND CONTRASTING APPROACHES

Experiential Approaches

Current practices in social skills training can be categorized into three approaches: experiential, cognitive, and instructional. These approaches can be shown to vary in relation to the outcomes derived, the methods employed, and the incentives used, and are described here to provide a backdrop to the more thorough explication of social skills training that follows. Specifically, social skills training as described in this chapter falls into the instructional category.

In this discussion, experiential is defined as those approaches, methods, and materials that emphasize placing the youngster into an activity that increases the probability of the occurrence of certain social skills, especially those that may already be present but at low strength. This approach capitalizes on the incentives that are naturally imbedded in the situation to reinforce the appropriate behaviors if and when they occur.

For example, Outward Bound programs, stress-challenge activities, and adventure education present opportunities for youngsters to acquire new skills or to enhance existing, low-frequency skills by creating situations with such high-demand characteristics that adaptive social behaviors are displayed sometimes without a great deal of teaching or forethought. During Scott's stay at the residential treatment center, he and nine other youngsters and two child care workers went on two outdoor trips, which involved backpacking and canoeing in undeveloped wilderness areas. As part of these activities, he and his cohorts were required to hike through a forested area with the benefit only of compass, topographical map, and enough food to carry them to the next campsite that evening. This activity had been preceded with some orienting instruction but did not teach directly the social skills such as management of conflict, decision making, and the expression of feelings necessary to facilitate the accomplishment of this group goal.

Furthermore, no extrinsic motivation was applied to the activity to reinforce appropriate behavior, but reinforcement nonetheless took place since food, water, dry socks, and other creature comforts were available once the course was negotiated successfully. In short, the probability of the occurrence of the adaptive social skills listed above was strengthened by the urgency of the situation. If the boys chose to compete with one another, engage in argument and conflict, or collapse into a helpless state as a group, they would not achieve the goal. Often in child care work, situations are similarly arranged that do not directly teach appropriate behavior but rather increase the probability of the occurrence of behaviors already existent in the repertoires of youngsters by reinforcing them as they occur. Although behavior improvements may be noted, this is not social skills training.

Cognitive Approaches

Cognitive approaches, methods, and materials present opportunities to describe verbally and analyze a set of events either real or hypothetical, followed by opportunities to apply the acquired insights directly to the events described. This approach capitalizes on developing understanding in relation to the occurrence of a behavior or a behavioral episode by verbally exploring the circumstances under which the behavior occurs, the feeling states associated with the behavior, the consequences of the event, and alternatives to consider in the future. This, of course, characterizes many of the psychotherapeutic methods, particularly the life-space interview and therapeutic group discussions so often used in child care settings.

At the treatment center, Scott participated in regular therapeutic groups in the milieu, in alcohol and drug groups, and in family therapy. These groups fostered the development of insight in relation to the events that occurred and the roles played by family members, peers, and other significant persons in the lives of the participating youngsters. Scott found support and trust from members in the group, which allowed him to validate his feelings and formulate possible solutions to the problems he was encountering. Further, he would receive feedback from the group leader and other boys as he tried to apply the solutions that he generated.

Talking through problems with youngsters is a valid form of treatment frequently found in child care settings, and can often be extremely gratifying and therapeutic for youngsters. However, this also is not social skills training.

Instructional Approaches

Instructional approaches, methods, and materials teach directly those behaviors the absence of which has caused the youngster to function in a nonadaptive way. One might expect to find the presentation of a model, opportunities to role-play, the delivery of performance feedback, and opportunities to try the newly learned behavior in problematic situations.

In the course of treatment, Scott participated regularly in a social skills training group conducted by child care workers. As an example, during one series of sessions, the group learned the skill of receiving negative feedback. Not only did the workers directly model the skill that was being taught but they employed a commercially available videotape to present modeling displays of the skill. After the displays were presented, the boys in the group were given opportunities to role-play the skill that was presented. This role-playing occurred over a number of sessions and eventually incorporated situations generated from the experience of the boys.

Following each role-play, the group would provide feedback to the role players as to whether or not they followed the constituent steps making up the skill. Sometimes feedback was provided by the role-players themselves, sometimes by the child care workers, and sometimes by members of the group. Reinforcement was also provided by way of program incentives, as well as approval and praise.

Finally, the boys in the group were encouraged to apply the new skill to situations in which its absence was problematic, or in situations that occurred outside the initial instructional setting. Each application of the skill was discussed during the next session and modified if the outcome was not satisfactory. The youngsters were also encouraged to use their newly learned skills in school, in family sessions, on the job if they held one, on home visits, and in other appropriate situations in real-life settings. This is social skills training because the procedures are instructional in nature and employ models, role-playing, and generalization techniques. The remainder of this chapter describes in greater detail the essential components of social skills training, related materials, and research findings.

ESSENTIAL ELEMENTS OF SOCIAL SKILLS TRAINING

Gresham [1982] suggests that this technology is comprised of three elements that can be directly manipulated by the practitioner: antecedent elements, consequence elements, and modeling elements. More familiarly, combinations of the following are typically found in most methods, materials, and systems that have a direct instruction derivation: (a) modeling, (b) role-playing, (c) feedback, (d) positive correction, (e) reinforcement, and (f) generalization training. Each of these components is discussed in the following sections. For the purposes of this discussion of the elements of social skills training, the skill of expressing feelings to others is employed. This skill has been analyzed into the following components:

- Identify how you feel.
- Compose how you are going to say it.
- Choose the right time to say it.
- Look at the other person, take a deep breath and show the right facial expression.
- Tell the other person how you feel.

Modeling

Most approaches to social skills training include the element of modeling or observational learning. This usually involves the presentation to the youngster of an exemplary version of the skill to be learned. Some approaches employ presentations of the skill on videotape or film [e.g., Hazel et al. 1981], while others require the behavioral exemplar to be presented by live models [e.g., Goldstein et al. 1980]. Regardless, the common theme of these approaches is that the learner must see the skill and its constituent behaviors for it to be learned efficiently.

For example, when a youngster in treatment needs to develop "expressing feelings to others," the child and youth care worker should arrange a modeling display for the youth that presents this skill. Perhaps it might be modeled in a group setting by workers or youngsters who possess the skill, or presented on videotape if available. In Scott's case, a videotape was used in his social skills training group to demonstrate the skill in its exemplary form.

In addition, workers should take care to exemplify the skill daily in their interactions with the youngsters in treatment, so that incidental modeling displays can be exploited in conjunction with the more direct training process. Goldstein et al. [1980], however, cautions the practitioner that pure exposure to appropriate models is often not enough to produce imitation. He further suggests that modeling must be "enhanced" through the selection of models that appeal to the learner, by application of personalized reinforcement for imitated behavior, and by manipulation of modeling frequency. More detailed explanations of modeling research can be found in Bandura [1969] and Kirkland and Thelen [1977].

Role-Playing

Role-playing or behavioral rehearsal is that element of social skills training that allows the youngster to practice in a structured and supportive manner the skill that has been modeled. This emphasis on the opportunity to practice and refine the modeled behavior is often in sharp contrast to those approaches that encourage the youngster to try a different course of action in problem situations through discussion and other insight-building techniques.

Modeling and role-playing go hand-in-hand. In fact, Goldstein et al. [1980] has emphasized that each of these necessary elements when used in isolation is insufficient to ensure effective maintenance and generalization of behavior change.

For example, once the skill had been modeled either by the worker or by a youngster already possessing that skill, Scott and other youngsters learning the skill were given opportunities to practice it. This occurred not only within the social skills training group but also individually. Scott was encouraged to practice the skill in a mirror and with peers as homework during free time.

Again, research suggests methods of using this element effectively by stressing the role that volition, reinforcement, public expression, and improvisation play in capitalizing on behavioral rehearsal opportunities. It is a truism in behavioral acquisition, as in music, athletics, arithmetical computation, language fluency, and so on, that opportunities to practice are linked to proficiency. The same is no less true in learning personal and social skills.

Feedback

The element of feedback is best discussed in conjunction with positive correction since they represent elements that are not always included, or emphasized enough, in some approaches to social skills acquisition. Feedback is defined here as knowledge of results (i.e., correct or incorrect) and is to be distinguished from reinforcement or incentive elements (although these distinctions are often blurred in reality), which are discussed below.

When the child and youth care worker takes the time and care to detail with a high degree of precision the skill to be acquired, it also warrants providing feedback with the same degree of specificity. This means that if the skill is made up of five subcomponents, feedback at least initially must be delivered for each. Too often, feedback is delivered in a global fashion that gives the youngster too little information about the performance adequacy of each of the subcomponents.

As an example of feedback, the worker might have said to Scott during the feedback portion of the session following a role-playing episode, "You're getting close. Now try to keep your eyes focused on the other person's eyes without laughing and show more interest." The feedback, which is positive and specific, is delivered in such a way that the self-esteem of the youngster is preserved while informing him or her which subcomponents were correct and which were incorrect.

Positive Correction

Positive correction incorporates feedback but also provides additional opportunities to try the skill again immediately following an incorrect display of the modeled behavior [Delquadri et al. 1982]. This tends to strengthen the association between the behavior and the conditions under which the behavior is displayed. Ideally, after the learner displays the behavior incorrectly, he is told that it is incorrect or what elements are incorrect, provided with another modeling display, and given an opportunity to try the skill again.

For example, to follow up on the foregoing example, the worker might have noted that the role-play was incorrect, provided another display of the skill, and given Scott another opportunity to role-play it. In some learning situations the youngster often might have to wait until the next session to try to make the correct response. Employing positive correction means that an error or an incorrect replication of the model really should serve as an opportunity to promptly try the role-play at least one more time.

Reinforcement

Reinforcement is defined as an incentive or reward and is to be distinguished from feedback, although the two operations are best used jointly. In most applications, reinforcement may fall into one of four categories: primary, social, activity, or token. It is a common feature of many residential treatment programs to have a reward system in place for appropriate behavior. Social skills training programs also incorporate a reinforcement operation either through reward delivered by the trainer or by the youngsters. Goldstein et al. [1980], for example, emphasizes employing naturally occurring reinforcers or self-reinforcement, while Stephens [1978] employs a performance contracting system to structure the delivery of reinforcement.

If social reinforcement were the choice, the worker might have said to Scott when he expressed his feelings appropriately in the group or in his day-to-day interactions, "That was good. You gave good eye contact and you expressed exactly how you felt. I could tell by the expression on your face." Or if a reward system was being used, the worker might have added, "You displayed four out of the five behaviors that make up expressing feelings. That was good! You've earned four points."

Generalization Training

Perhaps the most commonly ignored aspect of behavior change and treatment is generalization training. This means ensuring that the newly acquired skill is transferred to wider and more real environments. Baer et al. [1968] have stated that generalization "should be programmed rather than expected or lamented." In the residential treatment center, this not only calls for opportunities to learn new skills, but also requires strengthening the learned behavior beyond the training environment.

Many models of social skill training include components to ensure that the youngster has the opportunity to try the new skill in the setting in which it was problematic, or in a series of settings that approximate the problematic one. Goldstein et al. [1980] and others call this homework. It is an essential aspect of the education and treatment process.

Once the youngsters in the social skills training group display consistently the expression of feelings or whatever skill was being taught at the time, the worker has to be certain that these skills are being displayed in other aspects of group living, in family contexts, and in school. The worker must arrange opportunities for this to occur, and evaluate whether the behavior has been learned. In Scott's case, he committed himself to using the skill particularly with peers in school in efforts to resist peer pressure. He further committed himself to using it in his family sessions when he discussed his plans for his weekend stays at home with his mother. In fact, to facilitate the display of this behavior, his child and youth care workers used an unobtrusive hand signal (which was eventually dropped) for a period of time to remind Scott to use this skill in real-life situations.

ASSESSMENT OF TROUBLED YOUTHS

The social skills training approach is proactive in character in contrast to some more reactive approaches. This means that it is important to determine systematically, from the first contact with a youngster, what it is that he or she needs to learn in the personal-social area. Systems that deal with troubled and handicapped young people approach this assessment and treatment planning process in several ways. Some practitioners wait for deviant or inappropriate behavior to occur and then determine what course of action to take. In some settings this is an occasion in which to apply negative consequences or some other form of disciplinary action. Some review records often characterize youngsters in terms of pathologies. Other practitioners may employ assessment devices that identify negative behaviors in a youngster's repertoire and only then build a treatment plan that will serve to reduce the level of these pathologies or negative behaviors.

In contrast, the tradition of assessment and program planning that has evolved with the growth of social skills training methodologies identifies, as a first step, an array of personal and social behaviors that are appropriate for a particular population to acquire. A second step usually applies a process of systematic observation and behavioral assessment to develop a direction for treatment and intervention. Hops [1982] has detailed a collection of assessment procedures that are applicable to personal and social functioning, and describes at least two categories of assessment procedures that are useful in determining the level and nature of a youngster's personal and social skill repertoires. In the first category are the rating scale and checklist. Generally, these instruments enumerate a list of skills and the respondent is asked to indicate whether or not, or to what degree, the skill is present. The respondent may be a parent, teacher, child care worker, or even the child. In the second category is the process of direct observation, which can be conducted with one of two methods, both of which require an observer to view the behavior as it occurs. *Naturalistic observation* requires the observer to view the behavior as it occurs in the real-life setting, using direct measurement technology such as event recording, time sampling, or other measures. *Analogue observation* requires that the observer view the behavior using the same measurement techniques but only in a simulated setting.

In Scott's case, his personal and social behavior was directly observed during a preplacement visit to the center. Also, Scott and his parents were asked to complete a checklist of social skills similar to one developed by Goldstein et al. [1980]. In addition, the child care staff observed his performance in a number of natural and contrived settings, using behavioral definitions developed by the program staff, and employing direct measurement procedures such as event recording and time sampling to augment the information collected from Scott and his parents. Finally, the clinical and school records, which accompanied Scott's admission to the center, were reviewed to identify possible target behaviors. Typically, however, these had to be converted from negative behavior descriptions to the behavioral complement—behaviors that prevent the socially unacceptable behavior from occurring.

From all this information a profile was developed that characterized Scott in terms of personal and social skills—some that were present and some that were absent. For example, Scott lacked skills in stress reduction, decision making, and expressing feelings, while having acceptable skills in initiating social interactions and managing aggression, especially with peers. This planning process thus encouraged professionals to view Scott in terms of specific skills that needed to be learned or strengthened rather than in general terms of pathological conditions.

APPLICATION TO CHILD AND YOUTH CARE

Social skills training should be considered for inclusion in the skill repertoires of child and youth care workers. It can support the accomplishment of treatment plans for troubled and handicapped youngsters by prescribing prosocial outcomes. In addition, it provides proactive and humane methods for achieving these positive outcomes.

Child and youth care workers also enjoy the greatest opportunity in terms of time spent with children to effect change on an hour-to-hour, day-to-day basis, especially when compared to other professionals on the treatment team. This maximizes treatment opportunities, as well as the efficient use of the treatment dollar.

Child and youth care workers can use this methodology in the following four ways.

Conceptual Treatment Model

This guides the development of treatment plans that emphasize positive treatment outcomes. Usually treatment objectives articulated within a social skills training model are stated in the affirmative and specify behaviors to be acquired. The model that is used to understand and characterize the child can be directly translated into treatment strategies.

For example, when Scott was admitted to the treatment center, the child care worker assigned as case manager assessed Scott's social skills repertoire by administering a behavior checklist to determine which skills were present and which were not. In addition, the school records and clinical studies completed on Scott were analyzed to identify social skill deficits noted by other professionals. Finally, Scott and his parents were given an opportunity to contribute to the assessment process by completing a behavioral checklist.

These information sources were then consolidated into a treatment plan describing the social and personal skills that Scott would be given the opportunity to acquire. This model then served as the conceptual system for planning, facilitating, and evaluating Scott's treatment.

Individual Counseling

This influences the manner in which the child and youth care worker relates to the individual youngster in one-on-one counseling situations. Social skills training represents a nurturant approach to building and maintaining relationships. Ideally, the worker uses an instructional theme in working with the youngster toward treatment goals, as well as in discipline incidents by showing and rehearsing with the child the behaviors that need to be acquired.

For example, Scott and his case manager met regularly for social skills instruction in relation to critical incidents. While the other boys in the treatment program had many of the same skill deficits that Scott had, some skills could be best taught one-on-one for Scott, especially when he manifested this need in a negative behavior incident occurring in the course of treatment. The worker would meet with Scott, indicate the problem, elicit feeling states associated with the incident, help Scott describe the behaviors he should have displayed, model and role-play the behavior with him, provide feedback, and help design a homework assignment that would give Scott the opportunity to display the behavior he had just learned.

Instructional Groups

This influences the manner in which the child and youth care worker relates to the group. Social skills training is probably most profitably conducted in group situations. It should be underscored that it is within the group context that many of the nonadaptive behaviors occur that characterize this population, and it is within that context that the youngster needs to learn to function more appropriately.

For example, Scott participated regularly in a social skills instruction group. This group met five days a week for 45 minutes each day and was conducted by the two child care workers assigned for that shift. During a typical group meeting a particular skill was taught that represented the best fit for behavioral needs across the group.

This was the setting in which Scott learned such skills as using self-control, expressing feelings, and receiving negative feedback. It is important to note that in these groups the skill to be learned was modeled, role-played, and evaluated. Also, it was within this group that his homework was planned and processed.

A social skills training approach was used not only in the group described above but also in his family therapy group, in his drug and alcohol group, and in the special education program in which he was enrolled. The possibilities for overlap, cooperation, and follow-through were almost limitless.

Family Treatment Component

This enhances the support and resources that the treatment program can provide to parents. It gives the worker a facilitative technology for restructuring the learned behaviors or roles that each family plays out in relation to the problems that their youngster in treatment displays.

For example, Scott and his family were taught appropriate social skills as a part of the family therapy component. In fact, the same strategies employed in the social skills instruction group described above were used to teach Scott and his family more adaptive methods of dealing with conflict. Scott's mother learned to express her dissatisfaction with Scott's negative behavior. She also learned a problem-solving technique, along with Scott, to handle decisions that had to be made at home, but had earlier been troublesome.

MATERIALS AND RESOURCES

Although it is beyond the scope of this chapter to provide an exhaustive analysis and description of commercially available social skills training materials and resources, it is possible to present a few that illustrate direct instruction. These materials were selected because of their emphasis on modeling and role-playing, and their ready availability. The reader is encouraged to review Schumaker et al. [1983] for a more comprehensive review of available resources.

Asset

Asset is a package on the use of videotapes to present models of eight skills in adolescents: accepting and giving negative feedback; giving positive feedback; negotiation; conversation; problem solving; following instructions; and resisting peer pressure. These materials employ modeling, role-playing, and feedback procedures. The materials are expensive, but they have high production values and could complement nicely other materials and techniques in a continuing social skills training program.

(Hazel, Schumaker, Sherman and Sheldon-Wildgen, Research Press, Box 31773, Champaign, IL 61821 [1981].)

Skillstreaming the Adolescent

Skillstreaming the Adolescent is a program in book form that uses a direct instruction approach to teach social skills to adolescents: beginning and advanced social skills; skills for dealing with aggression; skills for dealing with stress; skills for dealing with feelings; and planning skills. It offers a discussion of the direct instruction approach, the skill sequence and skill analyses making up the sequence, and suggestions for implementation and behavior management. There is now a companion book that focuses on a younger population, *Skillstreaming the Elementary School Child* by McGinnis and Goldstein (1985).

(Goldstein, Sprafkin, Gershaw and Klein, Research Press, Box 31773, Champaign, Il 61821 [1980].)

Transition I-V

Transition I-V is a program in kit form that uses a direct instruction approach with younger adolescents on the skills of communication, problem solving, openness and trust, verbal and nonverbal communication, and awareness of values.

(Dupont and Dupont, American Guidance Service, Publishers' Building, Circle Pine, MN 55014 [1979].)

RELATIONSHIP TO OTHER METHODOLOGIES

Perhaps it would be helpful at this point to compare social skills training to the other prominent methodologies in the field of child and youth care, such as life-space interviewing, behavior management, and ecological strategies. First, however, it should be underscored that this technology can enhance the effectiveness and, in the view of this author, is highly compatible with them, both in terms of process as well as outcomes. Second, rarely are programs or professionals pure in the sense that they are characterized by a single unified body of theory and practice. More likely they are a blend of those techniques that best address the needs of the youngsters that the programs are designed to serve.

Redl [1959] incorporated the notions of "new-tool salesmanship" and "symptom estrangement" into the life-space interview (LSI) process. The former encourages the youngster to adopt new behaviors to respond to situations that in the past had been problematic. Similarly, the latter encourages the youngster to recognize that many of his or her behaviors are nonproductive and should be discarded. Granted that the LSI relies heavily on a "talking process" with troubled adolescents, it still sets the occasion for a teaching process such as social skills training to follow on its heels.

Behavior management systems employed in child care settings are motivational structures within which a social skills training program can be conducted. This is true especially if the system has been oriented toward the expansion of behavioral repertoires by the delivery of reinforcement rather than the reduction of inappropriate behavior by the use of punishment procedures. Many practitioners of social skills training use reinforcement operations in the programs and structures that they develop. In fact, social skills training is a first cousin of the behavior management approach, having common origins in the social learning theory tradition.

Ecological strategies call for the restructuring of the social and physical environment and suggest that it is as much the human service professional's responsibility to change the behavior in the real world as it is to change the behavior in the treatment setting. Social skills training methods include generalization training as the capstone of the treatment process. Furthermore, the social skills training process fits nicely in programs that teach or reteach prosocial skills to the dysfunctional families from which these youngsters often come.

It is obvious, therefore, that these methodologies can be employed in tandem and are not incompatible with one another. Simply stated, LSI strategies can set the occasion for behavior change, behavior management strategies can provide the incentives for behavior change, ecological strategies can broaden the focus of behavior change, and social skills training can develop the behaviors that have been absent from the child and family system.

CAUTIONS FROM RELATED RESEARCH

Although social skills training procedures are in their infancy, relatively speaking, a considerable and growing body of research has supported its use. Here we can only reflect on this research; Gresham [1981] has provided an exhaustive review of it as it relates to handicapped children, and the reader is encouraged to pursue it.

At least three impressions evolve from the literature in regard to empirical demonstrations of social skills training. First, the research clearly indicates that the future vocational and personality adjustment of troubled and handicapped youths is associated with personal and social adjustment. For example, mildly retarded adults often fail in employment situations not because of characteristics related primarily to cognitive limitations per se but due rather to social skills deficits [Greenspan and Schoultz 1981]. Further, evidence supports the observation that the personality development of children manifesting social skills deficits is compromised, with an increase in the probability of mental health problems as adults [Rolf et al. 1972]. These data strongly support the belief that troubled children and youths require social skills training as a necessary advance toward successful adjustment as adults.

Second, research evidence as reported in many studies [Gresham 1981] indicates that while social skills can be taught, generalization and maintenance of these newly learned skills cannot be assumed. Whether the problem lies in the manner in which these skills are defined and objectified or in the adequacy of existing technology to produce generalization, is not clear. Regardless, the literature suggests that practitioners take care to invest energies in broadening the range of environments in which the newly learned social skill is displayed equal to those invested in producing the skill in the first place. The criterion of success should be whether these skills work in the real world, not whether they work in treatment settings.

The third and perhaps most far-reaching impression from the literature concerns whether persons in the natural environments of these troubled adolescents have the necessary social skills to reinforce the improved social skills of treated youngsters. Data from studies of mainstreaming programs indicate that mere exposure or introduction to mainstream settings of handicapped children who have received social skills instruction is not sufficient to effect successful social exchanges and relationships [Gresham 1982]; similar findings have been reached by postdischarge research on children who have returned to their families after successful adjustments in residential treatment centers with varied technologies. Treatment plans for the reintroduction of treated youngsters into families and schools must first change to some degree the social skills repertoires and tolerances of these receiving environments.

SUMMARY

To reinforce the theme of this book, social skills training procedures represent another choice for the child and youth care worker and are complementary to the existing body of child and youth care techniques both in terms of outcomes as well as means of accomplishment. In other words, it uses humane and effective methods in an effort to develop troubled youths to the greatest extent possible. Social skills training is not a particularly new technology. It probably represents what good human service professionals of all vintages have been using for the history of the profession. What is significant about the technology is its positive, proactive, and systematic nature. Also, it is a body of technology that can serve the child care profession well since it empowers workers who have the greatest opportunity to interact with youngsters on a day-to-day basis.

Social skills training capitalizes on an instructional process. It requires the practitioner to determine what skills need to be acquired by each youngster and to arrange modeling displays of these skills. After these displays have been presented, opportunities to role-play the skills must be provided to the youngsters along with performance feedback. Finally, care must be taken to strengthen and generalize the skills once they are acquired. Such was the case in Scott's treatment program in that it focused on treating his problems within the context of the family, viewing their problems as social skills deficits that were addressed directly and systemically.

It is the opinion of this author that social skills training methods are a professional competence that should be developed in child and youth care training programs along with others such as case management, counseling, intervention procedures, communication techniques, and assessment. The evolving profession and professionals in child and youth care should work to ensure the achievement of social competence by troubled youths by teaching personal and social behavior directly as an integral part of the treatment process.

REFERENCES

Baer, D.M.; Wolf, M.M.; and Risley, T.R. 1968. "Some current dimensions of applied behavior analysis." *Journal of Applied Behavior Analysis,* 1: 91–97.

Bandura, A. 1969. *Principles of behavior modification.* New York: Holt, Rinehart, and Winston.

Brendtro, L.K., and Ness, A.E. 1983. *Re-educating troubled youth: Envi-*

ronments for teaching and treatment. New York: Aldine Publishing Company.

Delquadri, J.; Whorton, D.; Elliot, M.; and Greenwood, C.R. 1982. Peer and parent tutoring programs: A comparative analysis of the effects of packages on opportunity to respond, reading performance and achievement of learning disabled disadvantaged children. Paper presented at the Eighth Annual Convention at the Association for Behavior Analysis, Milwaukee, WI.

Ferguson, R.V., and Anglin, J.P. 1985. The child care profession: A vision for the future. *Child Care Quarterly* 14: 85–102.

Fox, R.G., and Krueger, M. 1986. Social skills training: Implications for child and youth care practice. *Journal of Child Care* 3 (1): 1–7.

Gresham, F.M. 1981. Social skills training with handicapped children: A review. *Review of Educational Research* 51: 139–176.

———. 1982. Misguided mainstreaming: The case for social skills training with handicapped children. *Exceptional Children* 48: 422–433.

Goldstein, A.P.; Sprafkin, R.P.; Gershaw, N.J.; and Klein, P. 1980. *Skillstreaming the adolescent: A structured learning approach to teaching prosocial skills.* Champaign, IL: Research Press.

Greenspan, S., and Schoultz, B. 1981. Why mentally retarded adults lose their jobs: Social competence as a factor in work adjustments. *Applied Research in Mental Retardation* 2: 23–38.

Hazel, J.S.; Schumaker, J.B.; Sherman, J.A.; and Sheldon-Wildgen, J. 1981. *Asset: A social skills program for adolescents.* Champaign, IL: Research Press.

Hops, H. 1982. Behavioral assessment of exceptional children's social development. *In Social development of exceptional children,* ed. P.S. Strain. Rockville, MD: Aspen Systems.

Kirkland, K., and Thelen, M. 1977. "Uses of modeling in child treatment." In *Advances in clinical child psychology,* vol. 1, ed. B. Lahey and A. Kazdin. New York: Plenum.

Maier, H. 1979. The core of care: Essential ingredients for children away from home. *Child Care Quarterly* 8: 161–173.

Redl, F. 1959. "Strategy and techniques of the life-space interview." *American Journal of Orthopsychiatry* 29: 1–18.

Roff, M., Sells, B., and Golden, M. 1972. *Social adjustment and personality development in children.* Minneapolis, MN: University of Minnesota Press.

Schumaker, J.B.; Pederson, C.S.; Hazel, J.S.; and Meyer, E.L. 1983. Social Skills curricula for mildly handicapped adolescents: A review. *Focus on Exceptional Children* 16 (4) (December).

Stephens, T.M. 1978. *Social skills in the classroom.* Columbus, OH: Cedars Press.

Trieschman, A.; Whittaker, J.; and Brendtro, L. 1969. *The other 23 hours.* Chicago, IL: Aldine Publishing Company.

White, R.W. 1959. Motivation revisited: The concept of competence. *Psychological Review* 66: 297–333.

White, R.W. 1978. "Competence as an aspect of personal growth." In *The primary prevention of psychopathology: Promoting social competence in children*, vol. 3, ed. M. Kent and J. Rolf. Hanover, NH: University Press of New England.

IV

The Crisis of Cross-Cultural Child and Youth Care

Gary R. Weaver

TIM: THERAPY OR BRAINWASHING?

On my way to a humanistic psychology conference in Honolulu, I landed in San Francisco to change planes. I had caught the red-eye out of Washington, D.C. and stayed awake throughout the flight. Flying at night always panics me.

Waiting for my plane to the tropics during the early morning hours was an exercise in endless tedium. This was the era of hippies, war protesters, "black militants," and somehow I expected San Francisco's airport to be different from Washington's National or Chicago's O'Hare. I looked forward to ponytails, headbands, peace buttons, and Afros, but instead found polyester leisure suits, nondescript business attire, and beehive hair styles.

Drowsy, bored, and disappointed with the universality of airport crowds, I slumped down in a chair with my carry-on bag securely locked between my ankles. It was time to catch up on some much-needed shut-eye.

"Got a dollar?" Someone was tapping on my knee. "Sir, could I have a dollar?"

I pulled myself up while checking with one hand to be certain my bag was still tucked between my feet. About ten inches from my face was a teenage boy with dark complexion, well-worn light blue Levi shirt and trousers, a red headband, and jet black hair that flowed over his collar. Somehow his thick, wire-rimmed glasses didn't complement this fashion statement, but then, these were the days before cheap contact lenses.

"Do—you—have—a—dollar?" This time he said each word carefully and distinctly as if I didn't speak English.

"For what?" Having flown all night in total terror to save money on airfare, I wasn't about to part with a dollar without some explanation. Humanistic psychologists are both human and frugal.

A grin crept over his face as he struggled for an answer to this complex, and somewhat convoluted, question. For a moment, he looked like one of my graduate students who had just received the questions for his comprehensive examination.

"To eat," he blurted out, obviously delighted that he had found the right answer.

The ball was back in my court. I was faced with continuing a conversation of two- and three-word sentences or giving him a dollar. The thought of bargaining him down to a smaller sum never entered my mind.

For hours I had carefully avoided beginning a conversation with another human being. Long ago, I discovered how dangerous it is to lean over to a neighbor on an airplane and ask, "How are you today?"

Now, however, I was ready for a conversation and this young man was the most interesting person I had seen at the airport. Perhaps I could lead him into four- or five-word sentences.

"Why should I give you money?"

"Because."

Not a bad response if this were a philosophy course. This young fellow would be comfortable at the humanistic psychology conference. He speaks Zen.

"Because of what?"

"Because I don't have any money. I'm a runaway from Indian school. My mother is an invalid. I have no place to live, no job, and I'm hungry. Please give me a dollar."

I should have stopped while I was ahead. The "let-me-tell-you-my-life-story" conversation I had so carefully avoided on the plane had just begun, but the challenge of trying to carry on a conversation with him could be the most stimulating thing at San Francisco International Airport. Humans are social animals and must communicate, which is probably why some of us talk to ourselves when there's no one else to talk to. I had at least two hours before my plane took off, and it was worth a dollar to hear this young panhandler's pitch.

"Who are you?" This question usually elicits a job description—people tell you what they do—but Tim actually told me who he was. He claimed to have grown up on a reservation on the West Coast where his grandfather was a tribal chief. Like many young Native Americans, he was shipped out-of-state to a federal Indian school where he mixed with boys from dozens of different tribes from around the United States. He hated school and ran away. His mother couldn't care for him because she had been struck with polio and could move about only with the aid of crutches and leg braces. His father had abandoned his mother before he was born.

Tim had been in San Francisco for nearly a year and was able to survive with handouts from strangers. The best hustling was at the airport where tourists were fascinated with his appearance. They were not at all reluctant to give a dollar to an Indian boy. And it was obvious that he had great verbal skills with which to pry money out of even the most hardened skinflint.

It seemed Tim was as eager to talk to someone as I was. Most travelers either ignored him or handed over their money, but few engaged in conversation. He asked who I was and where I was going. I explained that I taught psychology (a knee-jerk response—I told him what I did) and was on my way to a conference.

It was actually an enjoyable encounter, although I was fairly sure that much of what he told me was pure fabrication. Nevertheless, it was entertaining and certainly worth a dollar. After my flight was announced, I stood up and pulled a business card and two dollars out of my wallet. I will hand a business card to almost anyone—drunks in bars, obnoxious salesmen, lonely old ladies on airplanes. It is perhaps an overreaction to my labor-class family background.

"If you get to D.C., give me a call! Okay?" Fat chance, but it is the customary thing to say. Tim tucked the bills and card in his breast pocket, smiled broadly, and gave me a curt wave of his hand. "Have a good trip, Doc!"

A few months later, I was awakened by the phone at three in the morning. I tried to avoid answering the phone in the hope that my wife would pick it up and I could drift back to sleep, but she can usually hold out longer than I in this game.

"Collect call for Dr. Weaver from Tim." Tim! Tim who? I have no relative named Tim. Of course, no student who actually expects to graduate would call me collect at three in the morning. I accepted the call.

"Doc, I need your help. Remember, I'm the escapee from Indian school." When will I ever learn to stop handing out business cards?

Tim was in a detention facility in San Francisco after having attempted suicide by taking a variety of drugs. In California, it is apparently against the law to attempt suicide. He was placed in a hospital because he was found unconscious with his nose broken from his attempt to bash his head against a brick wall. The life history he gave me at the airport was entirely true. As a juvenile without a parent who could care for him, he was a ward of the court. The judge decided to commit him to a state hospital for therapy and counseling and he would soon be transferred. He could leave the mental hospital when he was deemed "normal" or when he was an adult and no longer considered a threat to himself.

Tim phoned me because he knew no other psychologist who might be able to convince the judge that he was emotionally stable and should be released. It was amazing how rationally and persuasively Tim presented his case to me. Nevertheless, attempted suicide calls for help. I suggested he cooperate with the court. He could then get good treatment, three meals a day, and a place to sleep. I assured him that, in my opinion, he would probably be out of the hospital and on the streets within a few months.

He pleaded that he actually did not intend to commit suicide. It was simply a matter of accidently mixing too many different drugs at one time. But I held firm and asked him to write and let me know how things were at the mental hospital. After about a half hour, he was somewhat convinced that going along with the court was the best alternative. He really didn't have any choice in the matter. He was transferred the next day.

Over the next month, I received two or three lengthy letters from Tim describing his experiences in the hospital. He was an excellent writer and intelligent. He felt that he was being held prisoner and the only way he could get out of the hospital was to allow himself to be "brainwashed." At first I dismissed his arguments as typical resistance to therapy, but gradually his position began to make sense.

The hospital used a form of milieu therapy whereby the peer group helps to determine the wellness and progress of a patient.

Everyone was assigned to a particular group of boys who would, by consensus, rate each other somewhere along a continuum from severely disturbed to normal. The criteria were based upon behavior within the group.

If a boy is perceived as withdrawn, uncooperative, given to explosions of rage, and so forth, he might be ranked a Level Five. At Level Four, he relates to others, but he is extremely closed emotionally, shows little concern for others, and is still prone to bouts of anger. Self-disclosive interactive behavior takes place at Level Three. On this level, the youth also displays authentic emotions such as breaking down in tears while relating a traumatic event in his life. At Level Two, self-disclosure continues, accompanied by affective communication, and the patient demonstrates self-control, insight, and altruism. Still, there is some uncertainty as to whether he can make it outside the institution. At Level One the boy is certified sane or normal and is allowed to to exit the institution and return to society again.

This all sounds reasonable and fair. Yet the very behavior that the facility considered normal was quite abnormal for an American Indian. Being self-disclosive, breaking down emotionally in front of others, and relating traumatic experiences are all equated with losing face, shame, and humiliation. Tim would never display this behavior before other boys in his tribe, and he certainly could never behave this way in front of Anglos.

In Tim's mind, this was brainwashing. He was being forced to give up his culture and adopt the Anglo culture. He had failed at everything—school, finding a job, even committing suicide. The only shred of self-esteem and pride he had left was his identity as a Native American. How would other boys in his tribe interpret this behavior? What would his grandfather think of him?

Tim was right. To gain release, he had to display the behavior appropriate for mainstream children in therapy. He had to act like a white youth. And, deep down, he knew he was expected to think and feel like a white boy. Indeed, this *was* a form of brainwashing or cultural oppression.

If a white youth were placed in an Native American group, it would be obvious that the expected and accepted norms of appropriate behavior would be inappropriate for the single white child. Tim was the only Indian in an all-white group, and the standards of normality were equally inappropriate. Furthermore, there were no Native Americans on the staff, and the entire institution dictated that mainstream behavior was the criterion of normality.

I phoned the hospital and explained to his floor supervisor who I was and how I had met Tim. I told him of Tim's concerns and stressed the importance of his culture to his psychological well-being. His worldview, values, beliefs, and perceptions determined a great deal of his behavior. The price he paid to be considered normal—to give up his culture—was a price no white child had to pay. Surely, the hospital could adjust its therapeutic model for these cultural differences. Perhaps some sort of one-on-one therapy would be more effective and less threatening for Tim.

"I've studied anthropology in college. Don't give me all this Indian crap!" The supervisor was unswayed and claimed he had already heard all this from Tim. All the boys were treated in the same manner and the therapeutic model was standard for everyone. There would be no exceptions.

I was then faced with a dilemma—should I advise Tim to give in and perhaps risk losing his self-esteem and ethnic pride? Or should I encourage him to fight to his last breath to maintain his ethnic integrity? A great deal of his anger was a result of his inability to adapt to the social group in the institution and his feeling of aloneness in a white world. Should he stop fighting the mold he was being forced into, or struggle to keep his self intact, including his Native American culture? He had already spent a great deal of time in "isolation" because of his acting-out behavior, which of course was a reaction to the environment and pressures of the institution.

I compromised. I suggested he "scope"—observe the so-called normal white youths, mimic their behavior, and realize that this is a strategy to gain release. This was not a retreat or cowardice, but instead, a strategic withdrawal. It had certainly worked for many prisoners of war and allowed them to survive and keep their sanity.

To this day, I think of the ethical implication of my advice. Was I undermining sound therapy? Or was the therapeutic model actually doing more harm than good for Tim? Was I being professional or was I simply caught up in the warped logic of a severely disturbed adolescent? Does one child's pride and cultural identity supersede the years of experience and research that must have gone into the creation of this therapeutic model?

Within a year, Tim was released. Had he not played the role of a white youth, there was a good likelihood he would have remained institutionalized until he reached the age of 18. In the struggle to maintain his cultural identity, he was probably strengthened and grew a great deal. He had found a way to keep his culture when faced with the overwhelming power that tried to take it away.

He eventually hitchhiked across the continent and lived with our family. There was no drug use or emotional outburst or depression, and no denying his Native American identity. He spent endless hours reading books on Native Americans and even worked at the Bureau of Indian Affairs. He was never brainwashed.

THE DEMOGRAPHICS OF CHILD CARE

In the next decade the numbers of white youths in institutions for troubled youths will steadily decrease while the number of minority youths will inevitably increase. The demographic trends clearly show that these institutions will be filled with a grossly disproportionate number of black, Hispanic, and other nonmainstream residents. At the same time, child care workers will probably remain predominantly white.

The birthrate in the United States, which has declined almost steadily since the first census in 1790, fell to an all-time low about 10 years ago and has remained there, below replacement level, ever since [Rensberger and Hilts 1986]. The overall national birthrate is approximately 15.5 per 1,000. For whites, however, it is 14.6 and for blacks, 20.9. The black population is increasing at a much faster rate than the white or overall population.

Were it not for immigration, the low level of reproduction would cause the population of the United States to begin shrinking before the middle of the next century. Over a quarter of the increase in population for the past few years has been the result of immigration, with most coming from Hispanic and Asian nations. Their birthrates are far higher and median ages far lower than the national average of white Americans.

The average age of whites is well over 32, yet the median age of blacks is about 26 and the median age of Hispanics is 25. The percentage of youths among minority populations is much greater than among white Americans. This steadily widening gap between white and minority median ages and birthrates will result in a disproportionate number and percentage of youths within minority groups.

Young men are responsible for most crime, and because of the sharp drop in birthrates, the number of young men is declining

[Rich 1986]. Minority birthrates, however, are not declining as rapidly. If the vast majority of felonies continue to be committed by juveniles, we can anticipate that programs dealing with these troubled youths will be drawing from a population that is increasingly disproportionately nonwhite.

It is not simply a matter of birthrates and median ages that accounts for the impending demographic shifts in institutions dealing with troubled youths. Black youths are often clustered in urban areas, come from low-income and single-parent families, and are exposed daily to social and physical deprivation. The pressures on their families are much greater than those on white Americans. They are more likely to come from broken homes, twice as likely to come from unemployed families, twice as likely to live below the poverty level, and at least three times as likely as white youths to be unemployed.

Hispanic families are also overwhelmingly centered in urban areas with even higher rates of unemployment and poverty than blacks. Their educational attainments are lower and they are burdened with distinct language and cultural differences that only serve to enhance their distance from the mainstream of America.

Thirty years ago most immigrants were fairly well educated and came from the middle or upper class of their own countries, especially if they came from non-European nations. The majority were professionals fleeing political oppression. Today, they are undereducated, lower class, and fleeing economic oppression. They tend to cluster in urban areas rife with poverty and crime. In spite of their traditional extended families, immigrant youths are also faced with enormous socioeconomic difficulties that tear apart the fabric of the family. They are often trapped between cultures, marginal to both the traditional culture of their parents and that of their host country peers.

Is it any wonder that minority youths may have more behavioral problems than mainstream youths? Even without the demographic shifts, we would expect that they would be disproportionately poor, unemployed, living in urban areas, and would come from families overwhelmed by socioeconomic stress. Regardless of their rising numbers and percentage in the population, these youths obviously are more likely to have difficulties coping with modern society. In the near future they may swamp courts, schools, and institutions that deal with maladjusted young people.

The staff members of these institutions, however, will continue to be mainly mainstream or white. The percentage of minority child care workers and other professionals dealing with troubled youths is certainly less than 10%. Fewer than 1% of all professionals in the field of mental health are Hispanic. Approximately 60% of all children in group care facilities are minority children, and yet the staff members of these programs are over 77% white [Krueger et al. 1987].

WHAT IS NORMAL BEHAVIOR?

Except for such extremes as psychosis and physiological disorders, normality is usually culturally defined as being like others in the dominant society. It is exceedingly difficult to quantify and observe values, beliefs, thought patterns, and perceptions. Thus, normality rests overwhelmingly on behavior. Those not behaving according to the norms of white, middle-class, mainstream America often are perceived as engaging in pathological or abnormal behavior. Yet true pathological behavior is socially and psychologically destructive, not merely different from the dominant group.

Most people unconsciously place negative value judgments on that which is culturally different. What "they" do is bad, inappropriate, wrong, or abnormal, not simply different. An American might say that "the British drive on the wrong side of the road," when, in fact, they drive on the left side of the road. Or a foreign visitor might tell co-nationals that "Americans eat bad food," when he really means that Americans eat different food than people in his country. This tendency to perceive culturally different behavior negatively is most likely to occur when people are unaware of the concept of culture and the lens of their own culture.

It is almost impossible to describe culturally different behavior objectively because we view it through the lens of our own cultural experiences. This causes us not only to select out that which our culture has deemed significant and ignore evidence that might contradict or confuse our simple perspective, but also adds an evaluative dimension where our behavior becomes normal, and their different behavior becomes abnormal. If we cannot describe the behavior of others objectively, how can we possibly understand or empathize with that behavior?

Sometimes that which is culturally different is not even given attention. It is ignored or denied, and other people and the artifacts of their culture are treated as invisible or marginal. This is somewhat like the tourist in Mexico who asks a vendor the price of a serape. "Three hundred pesos," the vendor replies. "No, how much is it in real money?"

Children who are culturally different are not simply viewed as different. Their culture is ignored or denied and the children feel marginal. And their behavior is often perceived as abnormal, when in fact it may be only culturally different. To illustrate, consider the following scenario:

> Gloria, a six-year-old, inner-city black child has been having difficulty in school. Her teacher, a white, middle-class woman in her mid-thirties, tells Gloria to ask her mother to come to school to see her after class. Gloria responds, "No ma'am, she be sick." What might the teacher think of this response: Gloria is not very bright—she is speaking bad English. The teacher then suggests that Gloria ask her mother to come to school next week, after class. Gloria again responds, only more emphatically this time, "No, ma'am. She *be* sick." Now, what does the teacher think? Not only is Gloria speaking bad English, she is probably lying. How does Gloria know that her mother will be sick next week?

All of the teacher's assumptions are wrong. Gloria is neither dumb nor is she lying. Gloria is using the tense of the verb "to be" to mean an ongoing process. Her mother is chronically ill. This tense no longer exists in standard American English, but it is found in most nonwestern languages and even Shakespearean English. Ironically, one could conclude that Gloria is much brighter than her teacher because she is quite properly using a verb tense that her teacher doesn't know.

The verb "to be" is the most common verb in so-called Black English, a reflection of the cultural emphasis placed on who you are—family background, age, relationships with others, and so forth. Gloria's form of English is a vital part of her culture and reflects a value system and thought pattern typical of many nonwestern cultures. To survive and excel in a standard English world, she must of course use standard English in the classroom; black dialect is necessary to communicate with her peers in the community. It offers a sense of belonging and in-group membership so paramount for the development of self-esteem. It is totally appropriate for Gloria to speak Black English with her friends on the playground or in the community.

The teacher is engaging in a subtle form of unconscious racism. Had Gloria grown up in Scotland and spoken a Scottish dialect with her peers on the playground, she might be perceived as very intelligent, especially if she then spoke the King's English in her classroom. Gloria has mastered one language—Black English. Her problem is learning another language—Standard English—and knowing when it is appropriate to use one or the other. An outstanding example is Dr. Martin Luther King, who would often give the same speech to a black audience in Black English and to a white audience in Standard English.

Gloria's teacher views her as deficient in language skills, while she communicates quite well with her friends. Instead of considering her speech as a bilingual problem, the teacher is unconsciously viewing Gloria as an underdeveloped white child. This denies Gloria the right to be different, it treats her culture as an inferior version of mainstream America, and the burden of cross-cultural understanding and communication rests on her shoulders, not the teacher's [Raspberry 1986].

Unfortunately, although the teacher may never voice her assumptions, Gloria is more likely than a white child to receive the negative nonverbal messages "you are dumb" and "you are lying." Some researchers claim that nonmainstream children are the most adept at receiving nonverbal cues [Mehrabian 1968]. If we treat people as if they are unintelligent, we may well create a self-fulling prophecy. Children, in particular, are likely to believe they are not very bright and, in turn, perform at levels far below their capabilities.

When asked a question, white American school children enthusiastically compete with each other for the teacher's attention by frantically waving their arms in the air. Not only do these children want the opportunity to be first to give the correct answer, they love it when the "smart" child on the other side of the room gives the wrong answer. It is literally a matter of each individual student in competition with the entire class, and there is only one winner.

Native American children seldom wave their arms, which may indicate to the teacher that they are uninvolved or don't know the right answer. Compared to the Anglo children, the Native American children may appear slow in the teacher's eyes. Among Native Americans, however, learning does not take place by observation of a skill immediately followed by a demonstration of the skill before others. In their group-oriented culture, one does not publicly compete against peers. Social harmony and cooperation are much more important values than individual competition.

The learning style and ways of demonstrating knowledge are different for Native American children, yet the teacher attributes uninvolvement and lack of intelligence to their behavior. Within their culture, their behavior is expected, accepted, and appropriate. Waving one's arm for attention, trying to demonstrate publicly a newly learned skill, and competing with classmates, would be quite abnormal [Philips 1972]. Who one is—a friend, a member of the in-group, a person who values social harmony and cooperation—is much more important than what one does as an individual. The ascribed status of group member supersedes earned status as an individual.

Conflicting Learning Styles and Thought Patterns

What one learns and how one learns is culturally determined [Hall 1976], yet most people assume everyone learns the same things in the same ways as they do. Each culture teaches its members to solve problems and think in similar patterns that are specific to that particular culture. Nevertheless, most people assume everyone thinks the same way. If people do not think the way you do, they are often viewed as pathological thinkers. They are "immature," "ignorant," "unintelligent," and "uneducated." Not only is normal behavior primarily culturally defined, but so to are the ways in which we learn and think.

Abstractive, inductive, and analytical thinking and problem solving are typical of mainstream Americans. Learning is usually done individually, with an emphasis on precision, quantification, and the selection of relevant data to solve a problem. Most intelligence, aptitude, and achievement tests measure this type of learning.

There is strong evidence that Native Americans, black Americans, and even many white females think associatively, deductively, and relationally. The preferred learning style involves others, and there is an emphasis on generalizations, qualification, and bringing together all data to solve a problem. The mainstream style focuses on universalistic meanings and things, whereas the relational style features approximation, contextual meaning, and people [Cohen 1969].

These are simply two different ways of thinking and learning;

neither is better than the other. Most intelligence tests measure only "abstractive" knowledge and thought, yet many great intellectuals think contextually or in images. Einstein was a terrible mathematician and conceived his theories in terms of whole images. He had to translate his theories into the "abstractive" mathematical language and learning style of Euro-Americans [Hall 1976].

Children who think in terms of associates, relationships, or images are often labeled unintelligent or immature. Piaget believed that "abstractive thinking" was more qualitatively mature than "complexive" or relational thought. If we apply his model to Einstein, he would be categorized as a preadolescent thinker. Of course, most nonmainstream children would also fail to reach Piaget's highest level of intellectual development.

When these culturally different children enter the educational system, they are confronted with a cross-cultural clash of learning styles, especially around the sixth grade, when we notice a sharp fall-off of their performance. Often the family is blamed for not providing support or educational enhancement. The only significant change in their relationships with others, however, is their interaction with teachers and the school system. It is at about the sixth grade that "abstractive," rather than associational, skills become emphasized. Decline in academic performance begins to occur at this time for Native American and black children.

As these children begin to be perceived as stupid or immature, their self-esteem and confidence start to wane, and they may even begin to unconsciously doubt their own intellectual abilities. Is it any wonder that they might engage in acting-out behavior, given this assault on their self-image and the frustrations of trying to cope with a foreign culture?

Differences in thought patterns and learning styles are highly significant in cross-cultural education and child care; this is an extremely complex and unconscious manifestation of cross-cultural conflict. Attention is primarily given to behavior—to what a child does—not how the child thinks or learns. Who the child is—his or her internal culture—is hidden and ignored. And yet, who the child is, determines behavior. The conflict of cultures often creates the "abnormal" behavior of the nonmainstream child. When two cultural icebergs collide, the greatest impact occurs below the water level of awareness at the base where we find internal culture.

To illustrate these differences in thought patterns, let us consider a history teacher who asks students to write an essay examination on the following topic: "Discuss the American Civil War between 1861 and 1862." As the teacher reads through the essays he finds a paper filled with lengthy run-on paragraphs. In the middle of this essay, James, the student who wrote it, has included discussion of his father and the neighborhood in which he grew up.

The teacher confronts him. "James, you cannot write three-page paragraphs. You must organize your writing into a series of distinct paragraphs with a lead or topic sentence, subsentences, and a transitionary sentence that leads into the next paragraph. And your father and neighborhood are really irrelevant to the American Civil War."

James is a black child who thinks associatively or relationally. He ties thoughts together almost poetically and, in his mind, everything that is associated with the topic is relevant. His father is very much like General Lee in his demeanor, and a fire in his father's neighborhood created the kind of havoc and remorse that occurred as the North moved through the South. In a poetic fashion, James wrote of the "sad buildings" and "grieving animals." He was engaging in what Piaget would term anthropomorphic thought by giving human traits and feelings to nonhuman things, a clear indication of immature intellectual development in Piaget's model.

James flunked his examination, not because of lack of intelligence or understanding, but because he failed to think in an "abstractive" manner. What the teacher actually wanted was for James to consider all the lectures he had given and all the books that were read and select out or abstract that which the teacher felt was pertinent to the topic. James' problem was that he related everything to the topic and communicated in an associative style. He wrote his essay as a whole image, a poem, rather than a series of precise and distinct paragraphs. Perhaps this helps explain why poetry is so much admired in his black community. The teacher wanted an office memo, not a poem.

The style of learning that excites James the most is highly participatory in the context of a group. If he is excited about an idea, he wants to share his enthusiasm, and sitting alone before an open book does not allow for interaction with others. In church, when the preacher moves the congregation, they verbally participate by shouting "Amen" and "all right." Contrast this with the behavior of white Episcopalians in a suburban community.

The teacher perceived the behavior of his black children as

disruptive and a sign that they are not learning, when in fact, had they quietly sat taking notes, little learning would be taking place. If the teacher understood James' culture, including his typical style of learning, thought patterns, and associative communication, he would not make these negative attributions to James' behavior. Furthermore, he would know that James' real problem is learning another culture that has a different way of gaining knowledge, thinking, and communicating. James is abnormal only to the degree that he has not internalized the norms of the teacher's culture regarding education. In his own community or culture, he is perfectly normal.

Here is another example of where the burden of understanding and adjustment rests on the child, not the adult. A bicultural approach would lessen the probability that James would feel inferior, unintelligent, and academically incapable. James must, of course, learn to think and communicate in a mainstream fashion, given the nature of American society. He certainly does not want to remain encapsulated in his neighborhood community, and he does want to excel academically. But he is not verbally and intellectually underdeveloped or deprived, he is not unintelligent, and he is not intellectually immature. He is simply culturally different from the mainstream.

Cross–Cultural Perception

Picture yourself as a young, white policeman patrolling the inner city of a large metropolitan area on a hot summer evening. Gang muggings and break-ins have taken place in the area and most of the residents are black. You come upon a group of about a dozen black male youths on a street corner gesturing violently and shouting obscenities at each other. You overhear one young man shout at another, "Yo muther, she like a railroad track cause she bin laid all over the land!" This insult is accompanied by a menacing finger pointed at another youth who is rocking back and forth as if to prepare for an assault.

The situation presents itself as a potential explosion of rage and you step in to break up the group. Obviously a fight is brewing or the young men wouldn't be standing in the streets shouting insults at each other with menacing gestures. But is this the reality or only your image of reality? In effect, it makes no difference once you've acted, because you have the power and authority of being an enforcer of the law.

These inner-city youths were merely engaging in a friendly form of interaction called "joining," "the numbers," or "the dozens." Each one tries to out-insult the other, often very poetically, until the opponent cannot come back with a clever insult that is more sophisticated and poetic than the one given. The street corner was a meeting place, especially on hot evenings when the lack of air conditioning makes the tenements unbearable. And although there was little real hostility present during the exchanges, your intrusion would definitely provoke hostility from the group.

Lack of cultural understanding and the element of tension caused you to react with your rule of thumb, to judge the situation only in terms of your own experience and perceptions. Certainly a group of young white men standing on a street corner in suburbia and insulting each other would connote anger and hostility. But this is a different cultural milieu, and careful observation would have contradicted that assumption in the inner city. For example, had you quietly observed for a few minutes you would have heard laughter after each insult from the other members of the group and the menacing gestures would have soon appeared as almost choreographed, teasing nonverbal expressions and not actually spontaneously hostile movements [Williams 1985].

The average white policeman can draw on his own behavior to predict the behavior of other whites; he cannot necessarily do so with blacks. A group of black juveniles standing on a street corner shouting insults at each other regarding their respective mothers might appear as a disturbance to the white policeman, while to the average black it is an acceptable way of interacting that has little potential for violence. The white policeman has no way of predicting the behavior of blacks from his own experience, and he consequently turns to the rules (the system) to judge what is proper or improper. There is ambiguity—the normal cues to aid in judging the situation are no longer present—that consequently produces anxiety. Thus, he is tempted to oversimplify, distort, and perhaps even project his own frustrations and hostility into the scenario. He uses his rule of thumb, but his thumb carries much more force than that of the average citizen. The net effect is prejudice enforced with the threat or actuality of violence.

Cross-cultural misunderstanding is inevitable when two different cultures are interacting during conflict or high-anxiety situations, and most of the interaction is nonverbal. A gesture, the symbol of a gun, a shout—all can be misinterpreted and usually are

[Weaver 1975]. During a period of conflict, the need to act and react is most likely to cause us to fail to consider all possible causes and variables of situations.

It is much easier to generalize negative characteristics of another's behavior when we lack experience with and knowledge of his or her culture. The psychologist Adorno once defined prejudice as "being down on that which you are not up on." If you know the culture of others, you know their motives and you can place their behavior in the context of their culture. If you are ignorant of their culture, however, they become dehumanized, and are judged only by the standards of your own culture-specific experiences.

On one hand, when "we" do something negative, we often attribute the behavior to the situation. We do not normally engage in this bad or inappropriate behavior. On the other hand, when "they" do something negative, it is because it is their typical behavior. It is a trait of those people. "I cheated on that examination because the professor was unfair, but Hispanic kids are always cheating." This tendency to make situational attributes to our bad behavior and trait attributions to their behavior is a fundamental error in cross-cultural perception [Brislin 1981]. It is most likely to happen if we know little of another's culture and crisis or conflict is taking place.

To be fair, let us reverse our hypothetical illustration and imagine yourself as a black policeman who has grown up in the inner city of Washington, D.C. You have joined the police force of a small midwestern town that is predominantly white. As you pull up to an intersection, you glance out your car window and see a group of white teenagers jammed into a small car. To your amazement, one young man has dropped his trousers and has his bottom hanging out the car window.

This could only be indecent exposure and you arrest the young man. In white communities, however, this might be a fairly normal form of adolescent play called "mooning." Although it is unlikely you would ever see a black teenager engaging in this behavior, it is rather common among white adolescents. As a black policeman, your rule of thumb leads to the conclusion that this is indecent and, in fact, a criminal act. Rather than seeing it as a part of normal, albeit strange, white male teenage behavior, you might attribute it to the sexual perversion of these boys. It is possible that you could perceive it as an intentional affront to you—a form of racism intended to embarrass or humiliate the observer.

Here, "possibilistic" thinking is added to "rule of thumb" thinking. It is indeed possible that this white youth went out of his way to expose his posterior to you because you are black, but it is highly improbable [Fromm 1961]. Chances are that the youth was quite shocked to be caught in this awkward situation by a policeman, regardless of race. When we assume the possible as probable, we are engaging in a form of paranoia that causes us to become even more ethnocentric and self-centered. We cannot develop empathy for the other person or put ourselves in his or her shoes to understand the motivation for a particular behavior. We cannot put the behavior in the context of the situation or culture of the other person.

In child and youth care, days are filled with conflict and crisis. How often do child care workers perceive behavior of culturally different children in the context of their culture or the situation? Do we make trait attributions instead of situational attributions to inappropriate behavior? Do we apply our rule of thumb when we should be considering all variables to account for that behavior? Do we sometimes engage in possibilistic rather than probabilistic thinking?

Cross-Cultural Interaction

Each of us has a particular worldview or image of reality. When we interact with others, we often assume that they share our perceptions and give the same meaning to messages as we do. If we have few similar experiences, however, we do not perceive reality in similar ways, and consequently our messages have quite different meanings.

Our perceptions influence our thought patterns, values, and beliefs, which, in turn, influence our perceptions [Singer 1987]. We act and react according to our image of reality. To this extent, our perception or image of reality, not reality itself, is what determines behavior, including our interactions with others. While some might view all human interactions as an opportunity for competition, others might view them as opportunities for cooperation. Sitting alone in a cafeteria because we seek privacy might be perceived by others as being aloof, hostile, or arrogant.

The meaning we give to messages is determined by our experiences or culture. We do not send meaning, we send messages. If we have experienced the world in similar ways, then our messages will elicit similar meanings. Meanings are in our head. If I sit facing an old Arab with my ankle on my knee and the bottom of my shoe exposed to his view, he would be highly insulted. The sole of my shoe touches the earth, which is filthy and, in his culture, I am exposing my filthy shoe to his face. In the United States, this is a typically macho way of sitting, and the bottom of one's shoe has no particular meaning.

If I am speaking to the Arab gentleman, it is highly unlikely he is paying attention to a word I am saying, because he has been programmed by his culture to attend to this shocking message—"bottom of shoe in my face." The verbal messages I am sending are not getting through because they are overwhelmed by my strong nonverbal message. Further, in his culture, people are generally more aware of nonverbal messages than in the mainstream American culture. Imagine yourself talking to someone who has his finger in his nose and is speaking to you; chances are you would not pay much attention to what he is saying.

Our culture teaches us what messages to attend to and what those messages mean. This is especially true of nonverbal messages, because their meanings are almost entirely culture-specific. Moreover, we learn how to communicate nonverbally simply by growing up and participating with others in the culture. Verbal communication is learned formally, explicitly, in the classroom, while nonverbal communication is learned informally, implicitly, through interaction with others. Because nonverbal communication skills are unconsciously acquired, most of us are unaware that we are constantly sending and receiving these messages and giving them meanings.

One researcher found that in face-to-face interaction perhaps 90% of the messages we send that communicate feelings are sent nonverbally—by our facial expression, tone of voice, posture, gesture, and spatial distance [Mehrabian 1968]. The meanings we unconsciously give to these messages are almost entirely based upon experiences in our own culture. If simultaneous verbal and nonverbal messages are contradictory, the nonverbal messages have greater credibility. For example, most of us have left an interview feeling that we know we will not get the job, although the interviewer may have given rather positive assurances we might have the job. In all likelihood, the interviewer's face, tone of voice, or gestures told us that we were not going to be hired and these messages were much more powerful than the verbal assurances.

Nonverbal messages have such unconsciously attributed culture-specific affective meaning that they are a major source of communications breakdown between people of different cultures. When Jesse Jackson chants "I AM SOMEBODY!" and involves the audience in repeating the chant, many whites are repulsed and equate this emotionalism and audience participation with loss of control, demogoguery, and manipulation. Blacks tend to perceive Jackson as a powerful speaker whose sincerity is demonstrated by his emotional style. Audience participation is an indication that he is in tune with all present, as when a black minister's moving sermon elicits shouts of "AMEN!" from the congregation.

According to linguist Thomas Kochman, "blacks treasure boldness and audacity as signs of leadership ability, while in 'mainstream American politics,' boldness and audacity are taken to mean an individual is not stable, not a team player" [Williams 1985]. Blacks also make a distinction between arguing and fighting that whites do not. For blacks, verbal confrontation can go a long way before physical confrontation is threatened. Arguing with emotive boldness is a way of truth seeking. A person who will not confront another about a problem is not concerned and does not attach importance to either the problem or the other person involved. Thus, in an argument, whites think "fight" long before blacks do.

In child and youth care, how often do white workers give the meaning "fight" to a message sent by a black coworker or child that was intended to mean "I care," "I feel strongly about this," or "I sincerely want to resolve this matter?" Child care workers often seek to keep a lid on situations, yet how many times do they use preemptive force to stop a "fight" that may be merely a verbal confrontation? Is a child or coworker perceived as unstable or out of control simply because he or she uses a different style of communication?

Conversely, how are white child care workers perceived by their black coworkers and children when they respond to a bold, emotional statement with cool, unemotional words? Is it any wonder that some whites are viewed as inhuman or insincere when they may feel they are only being professional, rational, and in control?

If a conflict does take place, when do we begin to negotiate? Among Hispanics, disputes follow steps or chains that are different from those of Anglos [Hall 1976]. Because of the high premium placed upon social harmony, Hispanics may not speak out when they are first offended. After many such slights, however, they seem to explode uncontrollably. This indicates "I can't take it anymore. I'm upset. Let's talk about it." The emotional outburst may be the first verbalization that something is wrong. Furthermore, it sets the stage for negotiation because all the cards are on the table.

To an Anglo-American, the outburst is equated with loss of control, irrationality, and fight. He may feel the Hispanic ought to have spoken up when the first offense occurred rather than waiting until there is no possibility of rational discussion. At the very moment when the Hispanic wants to discuss a problem, the Anglo-American thinks the dispute has gone well beyond the discussion stage. During the Malvinas or Falkland Island War between Britain and Argentina, the Argentines were genuinely perplexed when the British refused to negotiate once the fighting had begun. From Argentina's perspective, the British were being totally unreasonable [Travis 1985].

In a child care facility, white counselors may appear unreasonable to Hispanic children when they refuse to negotiate once a lively and emotional verbal exchange has taken place. Black children might not even see a need to negotiate because the situation is not actually a fight, it is only an impassioned discussion.

How one resolves a conflict is also culture-specific. For example, among Asians, Arabs, Hispanics, and Africans, great store is placed in not losing face or being shamed. If a conflict is actually taking place before others, it is very difficult for either party to back off. Thus, third party intermediaries are often essential, and it is assumed that members of one's in-group will step in to mediate, thereby preventing the disputants from losing face. These intermediaries must be perceived as connected or related to the combatants. In a family dispute, another member of the family might play this role, but not a stranger.

Anglo-Americans rather believe that it is the responsibility of the disputants to settle matters among themselves. Third parties ought not to get involved and are not really responsible for what happens. This is somewhat like the old Spencer Tracy movies where the juveniles punch each other out as the good father or priest stands by to be sure no other children get involved.

A child who comes from a culture where the community and family act as intermediaries may assume that he can allow the dispute to escalate verbally because an intermediary will step in before blows are thrown. A child who comes from a culture where intermediaries do not play a part in conflict, however, may feel the intermediaries are interfering. Even when intermediaries are expected to play a part, how they play that part and in what relationship they are to the disputants are all important variables.

Generally, nonmainstream children are much more adept at reading nonverbal cues than mainstream children and their verbal and nonverbal messages can be fully understood only if one knows their cultural background. Mainstream children rely much more on direct verbal communication where the meanings of messages are not so embedded in the context of the culture. Unless we understand the culture of another person, it is extremely difficult to send and receive messages that have parallel meanings. During a conflict situation, we are most likely to give meaning to messages based upon our own cultural understandings. Thus, we often exacerbate a conflict rather than help to resolve it.

Because attitudes and feelings are primarily communicated nonverbally and the meanings we give to nonverbal messages are mostly unconscious and culture-specific, a great deal of attention must be given to how and what we communicate without using words. Consider the following illustration [Kochman 1971]:

> Jose is an 11-year-old Puerto Rican child who is constantly chatting with the female student sitting next to him in his classroom. Almost daily his Anglo female teacher must remind him to stop talking during class. One morning, however, she is upset by a personal problem before entering the classroom, and she has grown annoyed by having to constantly remind Jose to stop talking to the girl. As the class begins, Jose leans over to whisper something to his friend and the teacher decides it is time to stop this behavior once and for all. She yells out, "Jose! How many times do I have to tell you to be quiet when I'm speaking?" As she is admonishing Jose, Jose looks down at the floor and mutters, "Yes, ma'am." The teacher approaches Jose, grabs him by the chin, and pulls his face toward hers. "Look at me when I'm talking to you," she shouts, and continues to lecture him on how rude and distracting his behavior has been over the past school year.

Jose will probably hate this teacher for the rest of his life, yet she may have no idea that he feels this way. Although she may regret losing her temper, the incident was rather straightforward and Jose was the offending party, not she. As she spoke to him, he looked away to avoid her reprimand. She, in turn, grabbed his chin to force him to look at her for a few seconds so that he fully understood and paid attention to what she was saying.

Jose was sorry to have provoked her outburst and he did what many Puerto Rican children are expected to do when being reprimanded by an adult—he looked down at the floor. This is polite behavior in his culture and demonstrates that he knows he is wrong. To look an adult in the eye while being reprimanded is to assume defiance. This is also true in many other parts of the world including sections of Asia and Africa. The behavior that the teacher viewed as avoidance of wrongdoing and a deserved reprimand was, in Jose's culture, an acceptance of the wrongdoing and reprimand.

The teacher then grabbed his chin. At the age of 11, Jose perceived himself not as a child, but rather, a young man. To grab a man's face is a serious violation of his sense of masculinity, especially when done by a female who is not a member of the family or who is quite old. The teacher humiliated Jose in front of his peers and the girl he was so fond of talking with. Of course, had he done something very bad at home, his mother might grab his chin. But in this case he did not burn down the school, he had just tried to communicate politeness and accept his responsibility for what had happened, and the teacher not only rejected his efforts, she escalated the incident by treating him like a child and offending his sense of machismo.

It is understandable that a child would not comprehend the breakdown of communication that has occurred in this illustration. Note, however, that the burden of understanding is placed on Jose, not his teacher. If the teacher had a class with large numbers of Puerto Rican children, it would be reasonable to expect her to know something of their culture, including their ways of communicating. The same would be true of a white teacher with a majority of black, Native American, or Asian children.

If the misunderstandings have not completely alienated these children, they are eventually expected to fit into the mold of appropriate behavior dictated by the teacher's culture. As they grow older, they learn what meanings the teacher intended, and they learn his or her verbal and nonverbal language. The anger and hurt probably were caused when they were very young and, over time, they may forget what incidents caused these feelings. Nevertheless, as young adults they still resent Anglo teachers and think of school as something painful. They may not know why their white teachers aroused hostile feelings, but those feelings do not simply go away with time. Rather, they seem to build up and fester, ready to explode at any moment of confrontation with a white authority figure [Rubin 1969].

CHILD AND YOUTH CARE INSTITUTIONS AS COOKIE CUTTERS

How often do child care professionals view behavior that is simply culturally different from the mainstream as abnormal, or even worse, pathological? Do child care workers verbally or nonverbally communicate negative judgments to children, thereby creating a self-fulfilling prophecy? Are children getting "better" by behaving like mainstream children? Are we controlling, manipulating, and shaping minority behavior to fit our own conception of the mainstream world without regard to the price children must pay to become "normal" by giving up their own culture? If so, we are engaging in cultural oppression, or trying to bring about cultural homogenization—all in the name of caring and helping.

Does the average child care worker really understand who the nonmainstream children are—their culture, values, beliefs, thought patterns, and worldview? Certainly in child and youth care the emphasis is more on doing than being, and the deficit hypothesis is the underlying principle in dealing with minority children. What children do is all important and the child care worker is often paid to observe, control, manipulate, and shape behavior. Of course, fairness means that behavior ought to be regulated with consistency and standardization. All should behave in the same way, and all should be treated equally—but by whose standards?

Today there is a backlash against cultural diversity in education and child and youth care. Affirmative action, cultural identity programs, bilingual and bicultural education, and most community programs that accentuate cultural differences have been cut back or abandoned. "Colorblindness" and the deficit hypothesis have a special impact on child and youth care because of their overemphasis on behavior at the expense of identity or internal culture.

Since children may end up in a center because of nonmainstream behavior, and normality depends on their behaving in a mainstream manner, therapy becomes nothing more than getting them to fit the dominant mold. And this is all done "for the good of the child." The process is not one of throwing their culture into the melting pot of a pluralistic child care institution. It is one of forcing the child to fit into the cookie cutter mold with a white, Protestant, male, Anglo-Saxon shape.

> An 11-year-old Guatemalan boy by the name of Jesus was admitted to an institution for emotionally disturbed children because of his inability to control his temper in his suburban school and his acting-out behavior. His command of English was good, although he had a heavy accent. Before joining the other children on the athletic field, he met with the center's secretary to be certain all his papers were in order. She felt that Jesus was a strange name that would cause him to be teased. Thus, from that moment on he was known as Jess, a name he couldn't pronounce and that did not sound similar to Jesus in Spanish. As he walked onto the athletic field, he had a new name. How quickly one loses identity in the United States! In Guatemala one's name is seldom altered and, in fact, one usually has a name that includes both the father and mother's family name.
>
> Jesus didn't just walk onto the athletic field—he strutted onto the field. He knew he was the oldest boy in the center, and he was the eldest son in his family. His age gave him an ascribed status and role and he had to carry himself in accordance with that role. He was not simply one of the children, he was the young man of the institution. He would not allow other children to beat him in any sport and he took no guff from them. Even the college students who were his counselors were treated as equals, in that he looked them directly in the eye when they spoke to him, and he would not tolerate being spoken to as a child.
>
> His behavior was interpreted by many of the staff members as arrogant, cocky, and defiant. Some felt that he needed to have this taken out of him, for his own good. When he got into a fight with two or more boys, some counselors would briefly turn their heads in hopes that Jesus would get the "wind knocked out of his sails": what he needed was some humility.

Of course, Jesus was behaving in a fairly normal way for a Guatemalan, and other children would have accepted and expected this behavior in Guatemala. Jesus was acting like a responsible young man upholding the ascribed status given by age and sex. To allow other children to beat him in sports would cause him to lose face. To let the counselors speak to him as a child would cause him to be shamed. And his swagger would be in sync with that of other 11-year-old Guatemalan males.

Within a few weeks Jesus was given another label—"sex pervert." No one actually used these words, but he was discovered masturbating, and he seemed to be preoccupied with sexual talk. Further, he was caught in bed with another boy, and was placed in a private room as if he had to be isolated from the other children so as not to contaminate the institution. He openly bragged about his sexual exploits with girls in his suburban community, to the delight of the other children and the consternation of the staff. If his accounts were true, Jesus had more sexual experience than most of the male staff members.

One counselor was a devout Roman Catholic who felt it was his responsibility to remind Jesus that masturbation was a sin. With that admonition, Jesus got the message—he was a pervert. This self-image was reinforced by his having been isolated from the other children at night. Not only was the institution punishing him, God would soon join in!

It would be normal for a boy his age in Guatemala to be concerned with sex and to boast of imaginary sexual exploits. This is all part of machismo and would be understood as such in Latin America. And while his introduction of masturbation to the institution was a novelty for most of the younger boys, it was a skill many precocious 11-year-olds would have acquired. He was certainly no pervert.

As the children were lining up to take showers one evening, a staff member noticed that Jesus was not circumcised. For supposed health reasons, his mother was urged to have him circumcised. The meaning of all this was very clear to Jesus—he was having a portion of his penis removed because of his behavior. It was a Freudian nightmare for this young man.

His mother decided to return to Guatemala and notified the institution that Jesus would be leaving. During a subsequent staff meeting, the issue of Jesus' departure was raised and it was generally agreed that his progress would be undermined by the return to his homeland. One counselor blurted out, "Jess is American!"

Jesus had been in the country only three or four years. Certainly, he had not lost his native culture and he spoke fluent Spanish. Perhaps what this counselor really meant was that Jesus was almost broken—he was almost forced into the cookie cutter mold. Indeed, to survive emotionally, Jesus had become more withdrawn and less "arrogant," he had stopped talking about sex, and he even stopped wincing when others called him Jess. He learned to obey the commands of the staff and accept his punishment with proper humility. He was almost normal. He was almost mainstream American.

Minority Children Experience Culture Shock

Nonmainstream children go through genuine culture shock when they enter the institution's culture. The stress of entering this new culture is certainly as great as that of anyone adjusting overseas, maybe even greater, because it is not anticipated, the lack of control is more apparent, and children are neither emotionally nor intellectually as well prepared to deal with culture shock.

The assumptions regarding normality are mainstream, and most of the staff members are mainstream. Thus, the children get little support from others, especially the staff members, because the latter are culturally different and they themselves have never experienced culture shock. Children are not oriented to the dynamics of cross-cultural adjustment, they do not anticipate the difficulties, they already have emotional problems or they wouldn't be in the facility, and the cultural differences are extreme.

People who live overseas usually go through an initial period of stress that is related to the problems of adjusting to another culture. The most common characteristic is a sense of helplessness or lack of control. This malady is primarily a result of the breakdown of communication between people from different cultures; a loss of home-cultural cues as to what is appropriate behavior; the absence of that which is familiar, such as the physical and social environment; and the identity crisis we all go through when we are immersed in a new social situation.

Nonmainstream children experience pain upon entering the child care facility—the pain of being unable to communicate effectively; the pain of lost cultural cues that make life predictable and provide psychological security; the pain of struggling to maintain an identity in the face of overwhelming powers that not only fail to acknowledge their cultural identity but demand that they give up the identity and take on another.

Without role models to relate to, or others who can empathize with their feelings, the children often irrationally vent their frustration with aggression. Little attention is paid to who the nonmainstream children are, only what they do. And they are indeed trapped, with no control over their environment. They feel helpless, and the situation is hopeless.

When an animal is placed in a cage with an electric grid on the floor, it wanders about aimlessly. When the grid is electrified, its first reaction is to try to escape from the cage—avoidance, escape, or flight behavior. This is the most common initial reaction of anyone who experiences the pain of culture shock. Flight behavior manifests itself in many ways. The children may be perpetually sleepy. Much of the pain is a result of the breakdown of communication, especially nonverbal communication that unconsciously transmits feelings and is overwhelmingly culture-specific. Children take the ability to communicate for granted because they have been communicating effectively and spontaneously with others since they were two or three years old. Now everything is confused, messages are ambiguous, contradictory, or have no meaning whatsoever. They feel cut off from others. Sleeping allows them to avoid interacting with those who are the source of this pain.

The children may withdraw into their own world or interact only with those who are culturally similar. The withdrawal may be misperceived as hostility, and the banding together with others from their culture as an attempt to avoid blending into the dominant institutional culture. Teachers may describe them as slow or lethargic and counselors might view them as uncooperative or even severely disturbed. The staff members do not understand why the children are behaving as they do. Instead of attributing their behavior to the situation, they often give trait attributions—"He's got a chip on his shoulder." "Hispanic kids are always moody and into being macho." Or, "Black kids stick together and won't mix with the other kids." Sometimes the trait attributions are even more negative—"He's lazy." Or, "He's really a sick kid."

Of course, the children cannot totally withdraw from others for long. They live in a social environment in the institution. Let us place another animal into our hypothetical cage and turn on the electric grid. This time, close all doors to prevent any escape from the painful environment. Within minutes the animals will attack each other and eventually one will die. When any animal is trapped in a painful situation from which there is no escape or avoidance of pain, flight turns into fight behavior or aggression.

This is obviously irrational. Logically, the animals should attack the cage or the sadistic social scientist pressing the button, but instead they attack each other. Similarly, nonmainstream children are trapped in an institutional setting that creates pain. They cannot totally withdraw from others, and they cannot escape the institution, although they will certainly try their best. They feel helpless, everything seems hopeless, and they have no control over the environment or their feelings and behavior. The anger may be directed toward anyone in the institution. Certainly, children who are committed to lockup facilities leave those facilities more aggressive and angry than when they entered. The social and physical environment causes that behavior.

Sometimes the anger is internalized and the children become self-destructive. And, at times, the sense of hopelessness leads to learned helplessness and its consequent depression. Freud believed that one of the primary causes of suicide was anger that could not be externalized for social reasons and was then turned upon oneself. Studies of old people trapped in institutions where they have no control over their environment, contrasted with those who have a sense of control, show that their life spans are much shorter [Langer and Rodin 1976]. Those who could not influence decisions about when to go to bed, when and what to eat, or recreational activities seemed to give up on life and felt helpless. They were much more severely depressed and saw no alternative but to give in to death.

The autistic hostility [Newcomb 1947] and learned helplessness of the children may be interpreted as a sign of improved behavior—the children appear cooperative and calmed down. But from a psychological perspective, the children are in worse shape than before they entered the facility. Many staff members are simply relieved that the children are no longer exploding in rage, and fail to recognize the severe depression.

The pain caused by the breakdown of interpersonal communication is not relieved by withdrawal or aggression. If the cause of the pain is the ineffectiveness of communication, cutting out others only makes it worse. In an institutional setting, aggression can lead only to further restrictions limiting interaction with others. Again, the source of the pain is the inability to communicate. Because we are social animals, we must communicate; old people who live alone may invent others to communicate with because of this need.

That the breakdown of communication produces pain is evident when we lose a loved one with whom we have shared intimate communication. Or, as a teenager, perhaps we fell in love with someone who, when angry, showed it in a passive-aggressive way by not answering our phone calls or letters. We may have found ourselves acting a bit crazy or uncontrolled—pounding on his or her door at two in the morning, or even instigating a dispute to get some emotive communication out of the other person.

When we do something over and over again that gets rewarded, we perpetuate that behavior. When this behavior is no longer rewarded, we experience pain. The children we have been talking about have their lives—they know how to greet people, communicate displeasure, and begin a friendship. In the child and youth care facility, this message system doesn't work. Perhaps thousands of times we have dropped coins in a soda machine and received the reward for our behavior—a can of soda. Then, one day, we drop coins and no can appears. What do we do? I know many who would begin to kick the machine. It is illogical, irrational, and even childish. Although it does not get us the soda, we feel a lot better after kicking the machine.

When flight and fight behavior fail to alleviate the pain, children may become increasingly neurotic. This is a complex situation, and they may unconsciously distort and deny reality in an effort to remove ambiguity. This reaction might be termed filter behavior.

They might withdraw to those from their own culture and try to create a little "inner city," "San Juan," "Chinatown," or "tribe" within the institution. The avoidance of other children is often justified with dualistic thinking—"my friends are good" and "the white kids and staff are bad." The opposite also sometimes occurs. Nonmainstream children may reject those from their own culture and band together with whites. They try to deny their own culture and justify this behavior by thinking, "the white culture is great," while their own culture is "terrible." In both cases, the children are simplifying a painful and complex reality by opting for one culture over the other. They see the two as mutually exclusive and find no area of overlap or compromise.

When we enter another culture, we feel like fish out of water. Cues that made us feel comfortable are absent. Faces are different, people communicate differently, the food is different, and there is a genuine object loss. Problem-solving approaches that worked all our lives no longer seem to work, and we begin to doubt our ability to function in this new social environment. Our resultant confusion, anger, and depression are reactions to the stress of cross-cultural adjustment—it is situational, not chronic. Yet it appears as if the misery will never end, and even worse, nobody seems to be concerned about us [Weaver 1986].

As nonmainstream children go through the various stages of culture shock, staff members not only fail to understand the situational nature of the children's behavior, they compound the stress by reacting to the children's reactions, creating a "conflict cycle" [Long and Duffner 1980] and power struggle. The dominant culture will eventually win out and as the children's behavior changes, their values and beliefs may slowly begin to change. The dissonance between their newly imposed behavior and their old values and beliefs will only add to their frustrations. They cannot deny the behavioral changes. The only thing that can change to bring about consonance is their belief and value system [Festinger 1957]. Like Winston Smith in *1984*, they may even begin to love "Big Brother" and hate themselves.

High Recidivism of Minority Youth

After the children are released from the child care facility to reenter their community, in theory it's all uphill. They are deemed normal or well adjusted. Minority children, however, are much more likely than the mainstream child to return soon to the facility. The recidivism rate of minority children is much higher than that of mainstream children.

When they return, the debate within the facility often revolves around two basic positions. Some argue that the children were released too early. Others just as vehemently bemoan how the bad community ruined all of their good work. At times, a mixture of these two positions is taken. The children and/or their community are to blame. Seldom does one question whether the child care facility itself bears some responsibility.

In all probability, the children went through reentry/transition stress or reverse culture shock [Weaver 1987] when they tried to readjust to their home culture. They learned the behaviors, values, and beliefs of the mainstream culture. That is, they acculturated to the facility or would have never been released and considered normal. If they were returning to a mainstream community, indeed they were better prepared to function and cope with the world than before they entered the facility, but the very behavior that was appropriate in the institution may be totally inappropriate or counterproductive in their nonmainstream community.

The process of readjustment to their home culture is remarkably similar to the process they went through in the institution. Again, a breakdown of communication occurs. Their family and friends cannot empathize with the experiences they have had in the facility, the communicative style they acquired is strange, and even some of their nonverbal patterns are no longer similar to the others. They are out of sync with their own culture.

Again, there is a loss of cues. They grew accustomed to institutional life—its food, surroundings, ways of solving problems and interacting. The identity that emerged in their struggle between cultures in the facility is different from the one they took with them when they entered the facility. The various reactions to the stress of their community set in and, before long, they are in trouble again.

People in their community are unlikely to understand what they are going through and react to their reactions, creating another conflict cycle. Distortion and denial or filter behavior are again present. They may deny the experience they went through in the facility, somewhat like the war veteran who refuses to accept the reality of his traumatic experiences on the battlefront. They pretend they never left home and were unaffected by their institutionalization. People who have not shared their experiences are not interested in hearing their stories and they are unable to understand them anyway. It is like describing and sharing the experience of a sunset with a blind person.

The opposite sometimes occurs. That is, the children might deny that they have returned to their home culture. An American sojourner who returns from a stay in England may speak with an exaggerated British accent, wear three-piece suits, and smoke a pipe while continually extolling the virtues of England and putting down the United States. These children refuse to give up the behavior of the institution and disparage that of their community. To justify this reaction, they actually believe that everything in the institution was good and everything in their own community is bad.

Minority children may join together with those who have shared their institutional experience and avoid those who have not. In The Gambia, West Africa, there is a bar where the "Been To's" hang out nightly. They are not members of a particular tribe. They have all studied overseas, however, and spend most of their time talking about where they have been to—some have been to London, others to Paris or New York, and so on. They constantly relive their experiences and avoid socializing with those who have not left the community. The "been-to" minority children can share, romanticize, and relive their experiences in the institution, and the group becomes an exclusive gang that cuts out the rest of the community. In some cases, the experience may be viewed as some sort of manhood or puberty ritual—"been to" a juvenile detention center.

As with culture shock, almost all of these behaviors are unconscious reactions to the stress of adaptation and the breakdown of communication, loss of cues, and the consequent identity crisis. When these youngsters go through flight, they may try to withdraw from their family and friends. In the extended family and in-group community, however, privacy cannot be won. It is unlikely that most minority children could find a place to be alone. Fight behavior is more probable, and it may be channeled to those who are lower on the social hierarchy or who present little retaliatory threat, such as members of the family or younger children. The returning children may be as confused by their own strange behavior as their family and friends.

Reverse culture shock may be even more stressful and severe than culture shock. One study of Americans returning from overseas found that over 70% felt that they had greater difficulty readjusting to the United States than adjusting to overseas [Mercil undated]. Perhaps the reason it is more stressful is that it is almost completely unanticipated. When we anticipate a stressful event, we are much better able to cope with it [Egbert et al. 1964]. When people go overseas, they worry about different food, new language, transportation difficulties, loss of friends, and so forth. People do not worry about going home and do not anticipate stress. Returning minority children do not anticipate the stress of reentering their own community, the loss of familiar institutional physical and social cues, or the new identity they bring.

We know of techniques for minimizing reentry/transition stress and helping individuals to develop coping strategies that allow them to control their reactions [Weaver and Uncapher 1981]. Primarily it is a matter of convincing returnees that they may go through reverse culture shock so that they can rehearse or anticipate the difficulties. For mainstream children, this is not a great problem because they are returning from a mainstream institution to a mainstream culture. For minority children, it is almost essential that the institution provide some sort of reentry training. Without this training, the children have a very slim chance of avoiding conflict with others and returning to an institutional setting. It is unreasonable and almost cruel to expect the children to understand the process of reentry, and it is cynical to blame them or their community for their failure to readjust to the community. The responsibility rests firmly on the shoulders of child and youth care professionals.

Those children who are most successful at adjusting to the institutional culture are often the least successful at readjusting to their home culture [Bochner 1973]. They may have adopted new roles that are not entirely welcome in their community. And their intense identification with the mainstream culture that helped them adapt interferes with their home culture identity. Often these children do not realize how much they have really changed until they have returned home. Thus, from the view of both the staff and the children themselves, there is little expectation of difficulty.

Both culture shock and reverse culture shock must be considered as processes that can be understood, and coping strategies can be developed that will minimize the severity and duration of symptoms. If the staff and the minority children can understand the process and anticipate the stress, there will automatically be a sense of greater self-control on the part of the children and an increased possibility of considering alternative behaviors to cope with stress. Without this awareness, the children become victims of their own reactions and lose control.

There is no cure for culture shock and reverse culture shock, but there are ways of minimizing their effects and using the experiences in a positive way. For example, children who successfully go through culture shock have a greater sense of self-control, a broader range of perceptions and coping strategies, and experience freedom from their cultural prison. Successful adaptation would cause the children to be more multicultural [Adler 1984] and flexible in their responses to various social environments. However, this type of growth does not come about without some pain—in this case, the pain of cross-cultural adjustment and readjustment.

Only if staff members understand the dynamics of cross-cultural adjustment can they help to make this a positive experience for the children. Without their understanding, it is almost inevitable that they will make it a negative experience that may seriously damage the children's sense of identity and self-confidence. Furthermore, the staff will necessarily bear an overwhelming amount of responsibility for the recidivism of the minority child.

THE NEED FOR CROSS-CULTURAL EDUCATION OF CHILD AND YOUTH CARE WORKERS

Child care workers must understand the impact of culture on behavior and the dynamics of cross-cultural adjustment and communication to better serve the nonmainstream child. To be an effective child care worker, it may be as important to study anthropology and cross-cultural communication as to study psychology. This is especially so if the demographic trend of increasingly greater numbers of minority children entering child care facilities continues.

We desperately need more minority child and youth care workers. The number has actually decreased in the past five years. Minority children need adult models to serve as ego ideals, to model cross-cultural interactive behavior, and to empathize with their experiences. White staff members and children also need these nonmainstream child care workers to break stereotypes they might have. Observing minority group members in the high-status role of child care worker makes preconceptions untenable and leads to the formation of more positive attitudes [Brislin 1981].

All child care workers ought to understand the concept of culture and appreciate the reality that they have been conditioned by their own culture to perceive and think in particular ways. The first step in understanding how the culture of others affects one's thinking, values, beliefs, perceptions, and behaviors is to understand one's own culture.

Culture is like an iceberg; only the tip is exposed. Behavior—or external culture—is the smallest part. To truly understand the child, we must go below the level of awareness and find out what is inside the child's mind. Internal culture, including values, beliefs, thought patterns, perceptions, and worldview, determines external culture, or what the child does. Unless we can understand the internal culture, we will mistakenly evaluate behavior based on our own cultural expectations. Further, we may make trait, rather than situational, attributions to the child's negative behavior.

The unspoken ideal is to be whitelike, yet the nonmainstream child is not, and never will be, white. Various studies of black children who had an increase in their positive self-concept and ethnic identity showed no increase in their antiwhite feelings.

Moreover, a study of severely disturbed black patients found that those most severely disturbed identified with white society, as opposed to their own ethnic culture [Jackson 1983]. Strengthening a child's cultural identity is absolutely no threat to the white institution, and it may be essential to providing the type of therapy most appropriate to the nonmainstream child.

It is equally important for mainstream child and youth care workers to appreciate the richness of nonmainstream cultures. If the child care worker views nonmainstream children as deficient, the children will pick up the message, even if it is not verbally expressed. Nonmainstream children are exceedingly sensitive to nonverbal messages and are the ones most likely to pick up the message that they are inferior. This, in turn, may create a self-fulfilling prophecy—the children will meet our expectations.

We know that the international sojourner must understand the process of cross-cultural adjustment to overcome his or her reactions and develop effective coping strategies that may minimize the stress of culture shock. Nonmainstream children should also have some understanding of how and why they react as they do. Only then are the children free to act, instead of reacting, in relation to the institutional environment. Only then do the children maintain a sense of control and understand that their feelings are normal and shared by others who have gone through this experience.

Certainly every child and youth care worker ought to understand the dynamics of culture shock so that he or she does not become part of the conflict cycle by reacting to the child's reactions. The burden of responsibility for cross-cultural understanding and communication should be moved from the shoulders of the child to the professional child and youth care worker. Only the child and youth care worker can effectively break the conflict cycle and prevent it from leading to a power struggle.

Simply helping children anticipate the stress of reentry to their own culture may be enough to greatly cut down the severity of reverse culture shock. They have already gone through the process of adaptation once, and the process of readaptation to their own culture is similar. We can draw from experiences they had in the institution to help them better cope with those they will encounter in their community. Many of the coping strategies they already know can be used again, but they must be prepared to use them.

The child and youth care worker ought to avoid confusing sympathy and identification with empathy. Sympathy may be appropriate in many instances, but it is not very helpful and gives no understanding of the child's world. Identification assumes the child care worker can be like the child. At times, this may also be appropriate, but it will not help us understand the child or meet the child's needs. Instead, we must develop cultural empathy—trying to understand the way the child views the world and feels about it. Only then can we truly understand the child's behavior and free ourselves from our own cultural biases.

Children from different cultures have different worldviews, values, beliefs, ways of interacting, and behaviors. To understand their behavior we must place it in the context of their culture. In the process, inevitably we will begin to understand our own culture and its impact on our perceptions, values, beliefs, and behavior. Awareness of our own internal culture is a fortunate by-product of cross-cultural interaction and awareness of the culture of others. At this point, not only will we be more helpful to troubled minority children, we will achieve the freedom to transcend it.

REFERENCES

Adler, P. S. 1984. Beyond cultural identity: Reflections on cultural and multicultural man. In *Readings in cross-cultural communication,* ed. G.R. Weaver, 168–183. Lexington, MA: Ginn Publishing.

Bochner, S. 1973. *The mediating man: Cultural interchange and transitional education.* Honolulu, HI: East-West Center.

Brislin, R. W. 1981. *Cross-cultural encounters.* New York: Pergamon Press.

Cohen, R. A. 1969. Conceptual styles, culture conflict, and nonverbal tests of intelligence. *American Anthropologist* 71: 828–856.

Egbert L.; Battit, G.; Welsh, C.; and Bartless, M. 1964. Reduction and postoperative pain by encouragement and instruction of patients. *New England Journal of Medicine* 270: 825–827.

Festinger, L. 1957. *A theory of cognitive dissonance.* Stanford, CA: Stanford University Press.

Fromm, Eric. 1961. *May man prevail?* Garden City, NY: Anchor Books.

Hall, E. 1983. *Psychology Today: An introduction.* 5th ed. New York: Random House.

Hall, E. T. 1976. *Beyond culture.* New York: Doubleday.

Jackson, G. G. 1979. The roots of the backlash theory in mental health. *The Journal of Black Psychology* 6 (1) (August): 17–45.

Kochman, T. 1971. Cross-cultural communication: Contrasting perspectives, conflicting sensibilities. *The Florida FL Reporter* (Spring/Fall): 53–54.

Krueger, M.; Lauerman, R.; Beker, J.; Savicki, V.; Parry, P; and Powell, N. 1987. Professional child and youth care work in the United States and Canada: A report of the NOCCWA research and study committee. *Journal of Child and Youth Care Work* 3.

Langer, E. J., and Rodin, J. 1976. The effects of choice and enhanced personal responsibility for the aged: A field experiment in an institutional setting. *Journal of Personality and Social Psychology* 34: 191–198.

Long, N. J., and Duffner, B. 1980. The stress cycle or the coping cycle? The impact of home and school stresses on pupils' classroom behavior. In *Conflict in the classroom: The education of emotionally disturbed children,* 4th ed., ed. N.J. Long, W.C. Morse, and R.G. Newman, 218–228. Belmont, CA: Wadsworth Publishing Company.

Mercil, M. C. (n.d.) Planning and conducting re-entry transition workshops. Washington, DC: Youth For Understanding, International Student Exchange.

Newcomb, T. 1947. Autistic hostility and social reality. *Human Relations* 1: 69–86.

Philips, S. U. 1972. Participant structures and communicative competence: Warm Springs children in community and classroom. In *Functions of language in the classroom*, ed. C.B. Cazden, V.P. John, and D. Hymes, 370–394. New York: Teachers College Press.

Raspberry, W. 1986. Black kids need standard English. *The Washington Post* (October 1): A19.

Rensberger, B., and Hilts, P. 1986. Birthrate in U.S. remains below replacement level. *The Washington Post* (October 27): A6.

Rich, S. 1986. Sharp decline in crime rates forecast for rest of century. *The Washington Post* (October 26): A4.

Rubin, T. I. 1969. *The angry book.* New York: Collier Books.

Singer, M. R. 1987. *Intercultural communication: A perceptual approach.* Englewood Cliffs, NJ: Prentice-Hall, Inc.

Travis, C. 1985. Interview with Edward Hall. Edward T. Hall: A social scientist with a gift for solving human problems. *GEO* 5 (March): 13-14.

Weaver, G. 1975. American Identity Movements: A cross-cultural confrontation. *Intellect* (March): 377–380.

———. 1986. Understanding and coping with cross-cultural adjustment stress. In *Cross-cultural orientation: New conceptualizations and applications*, ed. R.M. Paige, 111–145. Lanham, MD: University Press of America.

———. 1987. The process of reentry. *The Advising Quarterly* 2 (Fall): 1, 3–7.

Weaver, G., and Uncapher, P. 1981. The Nigerian Experience: Overseas living and value changes. Paper presented at 7th Annual SIETAR Conference, Vancouver, B.C., Canada, March 11.

Williams, J. 1985. Missing the message: Thomas Kochman on cultural crossed signals. *The Washington Post* (February 9): B1, B8.

V

Child and Youth Care Work with the Deaf: An Orientation

George M. Cohen

VERA

Vera rested in the infirmary. Her normally robust nine-year-old-body was weakened by the flu. Her bleary eyes caught the movement at the edge of her vision as she lethargically turned to see Kate entering her room. In her twenties, Kate was lean and earnest. She asked Vera how she was feeling, but when she saw the abruptness bordering on contempt with which Vera responded to her, she wondered how she could get Vera to accept her again. She had come to appreciate, to know, and to love this child, whose intelligence, maturity, and linguistic ability enabled her to dominate the group of girls for whom Kate was responsible.

This dorm group at the 500-bed state school for the deaf numbered 12 girls between the ages of six and nine. Vera was the only one who was the child of deaf parents. Moreover, the parents too had come from deaf families. She had a powerful heritage of deaf culture. She really had no peers among her group. Manual language had been a part of her rearing as naturally as spoken language had been to Kate's early childhood. Few of the other children had had any integration of a culturally shared language until they came to the school. They were essentially mute children of hearing parents who had become deaf before they would have developed speech (prelingual deafness). Their lack of the capacity to use or understand speech had gradually excluded them from their peers as preschoolers and in many ways from their families. They had been sent to the school to learn language and then through it the tools of our civilization. They were learning the most from Vera. Vera did not need to be an aggressive or pushy child to achieve a leadership position. The girls rapidly became dependent on her.

Early in the year Kate recognized Vera's position in the group and had become engaged in a careful strategy to form an alliance with the child. Doing so would enhance the experience for Vera, permit a rearing climate for the rest of the group, and enrich the rewards of child care for Kate herself. Gradually, despite Vera's suspicion and ridicule of Kate's sign language, her work paid off.

Kate had been a public school teacher who became restless with the routine, and for her, the enforced distance between teacher and so many children in the classroom. She liked to be able to be close to and know a child. Having been exposed to manual language through a girlfriend, who was the hearing child of a deaf family, she became interested in sign language, took a course, and discovered she had a language aptitude. Through her friend and her friend's parents she discovered the world of the deaf and the culture of a deaf social club. Given her aptitude, the classes, and a fascination with the people of this different world, her sign language competence grew rapidly. Kate considered returning to school to qualify in deaf education, but new friends told her that some experience working in a dorm with deaf children would enhance any future formal special educational training in a way that any number of higher degrees could not begin to approach.

So Kate, with her teaching experience, the richness of her own life and rearing, and her new language, left the classroom and took a position at the state school for the deaf. She was fortunate in the assignment, for her supervisor Pam did not limit her own work to issues of accountability. She was a rare person with a combination of conviction, wisdom, endurance, and nurturance. She was conscious of the necessity, and had the capacity, to care for and develop her staff in order to foster a rich environment for the children. As was true for Kate, her nature also required closeness, sharing, and growing. Both she and Kate were burdened with the mixed blessing of always needing to learn, of always seeking new meaning, new understanding, new views of their work. And their work was little handicapped people. What could have been a better challenge than these children who had been deprived by fate of language? Language is the loom on which the fabric of interpersonal relationships and human society is woven. Language links our minds to the minds of others, our feelings to the feelings of others, our learning to the learning of others, and is no less a means by which we view ourselves, our personal history, and our future.

But Vera had not been deprived of language. Her language was as much a part of her development and mastery as that of any hearing child. Because of this she was exceptional in her group. Moreover, her alliance with Kate was rewarding to her in that she acquired an adult capable of trust through whom she could expand her view of the world. Kate had become significant to her. Although Vera's parents were friends with some hearing people close to the deaf world, Vera herself did not own any of this kind of relationship. Kate was the first hearing person to become important to her who was not part of her family circle.

At the Thanksgiving recess her parents, however, met Kate for the first time, and by the time Vera was returned from the holiday they had made it clear to the child, to Pam, and to Kate that they disapproved of Kate, not wanting their child's worker to be a hearing person. They were as adamant in their position as parents who are active in civil rights or ethnic identity issues might have been. Vera's old suspicion and ridicule of Kate was renewed and intensified with hostility and defiance. Kate was struck with the message—stay away from me, if not, I'll make life hell for you and you know I can do it!

Kate could not compete with Vera for control of the group and knew that she would not succeed if she tried. During the ensuing weeks her feelings of hurt due to the psychological and personal loss of Vera became extremely painful for her. As a mother might do in anguish over an estranged child, she spoke with Vera of how she loved her and how she had her best interests at heart. She spoke of how hurt she was by Vera's contempt. These efforts only seemed to harden Vera's attitudes and provoke more active rebellion. Hurt and confused, Kate backed off, which resulted in less active trouble.

When Vera then became ill, Kate went to visit her as was her habit with any of her girls when they were in the infirmary. Usually her visit was welcomed by a bored and ailing child. Vera's rejection was extraordinary, and Kate was unable to pass it off with indifference. She tried to speak to Vera of missing her and missing their friendship. Kate did not see a bored or acquiescent child. Vera simply averted her eyes to cut off the communication, her expression signaled her contempt, her hands said simply "bug off," and Kate was devastated. Her concern and caring were not enough. What else could she do?

In talking with Pam later that evening, she was able to express her sense of loss. She discovered how powerful this was, how it dominated her behavior. It felt to Kate as if she herself had done something wrong and must find some way to compensate for her wrongdoing. Pam helped her to see that she had done nothing wrong, and to explore the profound feelings that created a distance between herself and the child. Perhaps much of the power of those feelings was not hers but belonged to Vera. They wondered what could cause Vera to become more hostile as Kate's feelings were revealed? Kate's vulnerability? Kate's hurt? Why wasn't love enough? Could it be that Vera also feared a loss? That Vera was vulnerable, that Vera feared hurt? It was as if Kate's love and concern for her was threatening. Maybe what it threatened for Vera was a loss. Perhaps it threatened a loss even greater than she was able to comprehend. Perhaps Kate was feeling that which Vera could not begin to allow herself to feel.

The change had come with the parents' objection to having a hearing counselor; her mother was the most vociferous. Perhaps Vera was denying a conflict inherent in the situation; she certainly did not appear to have internalized a conflict of love, agonizing over loyalty and alliance between Kate and her mother. Because it could become too powerful and threaten to tear her apart, the child instead placed herself in a position of external conflict with Kate. Kate's sense of loss and need to make amends had made things worse, but they also helped to expose and ripen the issue. If a truth in this situation centered on a hidden conflict, Vera's conflict, then that notion needed to be shared with the child, together with an acceptance of her having a serious and painful problem.

When Kate visited Vera the next day, she had the strength to insist that Vera attend to her, that Vera look at her and "listen." Kate was able to present her sympathetic view of Vera's problem. She saw Vera as having felt that she had to choose between Kate and her mother, and that Vera had made the only choice possible. Kate said that she had learned how important this was for Vera, and that it could be understood and that she would not want Vera to risk losing her mother's love. She hoped that Vera could find a way for them to be friends again, but could understand and accept the situation if that was not possible. She told Vera that perhaps her own painful feelings taught her what Vera was afraid of. Vera wept. They both wept. The conflict cycle had been broken in a climate of warmth and truth. Kate had had to experience her own hurt and explore it to see that Vera was avoiding extreme pain, which resulted in Kate's knowing what that pain would be like. Vera had actively rejected her caretaker at the school rather than experience the pain of inner conflict. Kate's understanding and acceptance had made it safe for the child to feel the threat of losing both Kate and her mother's love and feel her pain.

The interplay and conflict of a child's inner world of feelings and the outer world of relationships is a developmental process. It marks the growth of a more competent, independent human being. For Vera, Kate's intervention added to her growing ability to separate and individuate, having survived an exaggerated threat of loss of maternal love. Given Kate's acknowledgment and acceptance of Vera's conflict, the child could courageously yield her rigid defense against the fear of loss. She could discover that she was able to experience and survive inner conflict and that her relationship with her mother would survive, too. Her world could be an additive one, rather than one that would give only so much and then have to be balanced by having things or people taken away. Kate also learned. She learned that being flooded by feelings about one of her children requires that she explore herself and postulate what conditions might produce those same feelings in the child, if the child could have allowed herself to feel them. She learned that it is possible to present an emotional truth and process to a child without turning the transaction into a confrontation, which might exacerbate the defense. She experienced the personal and professional growth that she sought and felt more drawn than ever to the process of child care and therapeutic management.

The foregoing vignette is limited to just one child care issue, just one approach, and just one other member of the staff who helped Kate. The anecdote is recounted to demonstrate that child care sophistication and sensitivity can be applied universally. Children are children first and foremost, though they may be handicapped by nature or by lack of nurture or both. Applied principles of careful and deliberate caring and rearing techniques can help repair the damage and enable a child to grow.

BACKGROUND

Child care work with the deaf is not a new field. Over 9,000 children are living in about 70 residential schools for the deaf throughout the country. Many of the schools are state operated and the vast majority are state supported. The children range in age from preschool through extended secondary programs that might serve residential students through the age of 21. Enrollment policies at both extremes of the age range vary greatly. Among the residential deaf school population, about 30% are identified as multihandicapped, with physical handicaps and/or emotional problems in addition to deafness. Many children with a prelingual loss also have other problems stemming from the same source as the hearing loss. Maternal rubella is perhaps the source of the most notorious example of early multiple disabling conditions in children. Other actively infectious diseases contracted in utero, during infancy, or in early childhood can produce a variety of disabilities, often in combination with anything from severe visual impairment to certain kinds of learning disabilities, to hyperactivity, to aphasia (loss of the power to use or comprehend words). Since the greatest portion of the deaf child population became so in infancy or early childhood, due to disease, it is not surprising that about a third of the residential school enrollment is of deaf children with additional handicaps. The schools have separate educational services and living arrangements for the most severely affected of these children, and various combinations of educational and dormitory "in-school mainstreaming" depending on a child's abilities.

Nevertheless, the total population is in care primarily because of deafness. They are not "hard-of-hearing" youngsters; all have hearing losses to the extent that "the disability precludes successful processing of linguistic information through audition with or without a hearing aid" [Brill et al. 1986: 57]. The vast majority of deaf children have suffered a prelingual loss of hearing.

Hearing children understand some spoken language before they are physically able to speak. They begin to associate some sounds and inflections of speech with feelings and events and objects in their social and physical environment. Eventually they become physically capable of speech, gradually replacing action as the primary means of influencing their environment. Unlike Vera, most deaf children are born to hearing families using conventional methods of auditory communication. The deaf family naturally is using a form of manual communication. Their children, both hearing and deaf, are exposed to and are able to participate in a sophisticated linguistic environment. Deaf children of hearing families are usually deprived of an early accommodation with formal language in any form. Of course, their intelligence, curiosity, and bonding needs require the use of all available sensory avenues to perceive their environment, as with the hearing child in the hearing family, or the deaf child in the deaf family. However, they cannot even gradually learn the order, abstractions or subtleties of an oral linguistic fabric, the nature of which is beyond their sensory capacity. Deaf children in hearing families certainly learn the meanings of facial expressions, gestures, and other components of body language as applied to their care and nurturance. In fact, they may be exquisitely sensitive and responsive to the primary caretaker's moods via these indicators. But they are not on the road to the abstractions of language: the symbolic representation of action, motivation, explanation, goal orientation, and causal relationship, to mention but a few of the functions of language in human society. When early diagnosis has been made, however, some families have discovered the information and assistance to make the extraordinary commitment to become "bilingual" or use "total communication" in all aspects of their home life. Under these conditions their children have access to a linguistic system throughout their growth. Deaf children can learn their "mother tongue" for the same reasons that any child learns to speak and to understand. The language serves their need to be liked and to please their family, to accurately identify needs and wishes, share affective reciprocity, the abstraction of future and past events, the exploration of reality and fantasy, and the twilight zone in between. Language acquisition occurs when its development is most useful to children in the process of socialization. It becomes a function of the self in the sense that mobility is a function of the self. It occurs as a part of the total growth process. It is not taught any more than walking is taught. As children own their mobility, they must own their language.

The deaf educational establishment has been making increasing efforts to collaborate with hospitals and health agencies in using new techniques to identify deaf newborn babies. Many states sponsor outreach programs providing workers trained to educate families about deafness and alternatives to exclusively vocal communication. Unfortunately, many children become deaf during infancy and the condition is not recognized until long after the natural developmental language acquisition period has passed. These children are often not diagnosed until they are of school age, and the diagnosis may be skewed by a history of behavioral problems and of dullness. Lack of speech may have been viewed as retardation, behavioral problems as neurological. Since deaf children without language cannot tell us how they see the world in the words we are used to, they show us through behavior. How we interpret that behavior is the examiner's problem, and it may lead to misdiagnosis. This can happen in both the medical and the educational fields, though the frequency of gross misdiagnosis has dramatically decreased in recent years.

THE RESIDENTIAL SCHOOL

Residential schools for the deaf have developed partly out of the need to best serve the sparsely distributed deaf population by concentrating and bringing together the professionals who have specialized and uncommon teaching and language skills and deaf students collected from large geographical areas. This obvious purpose stems from a strict academic objective: get the talent and training focused to serve the population in need of specialization. The residential aspect is a consequence of the need to collect a critical mass of students from a given geographical area. However much the absence of language interferes with socialization and interpersonal relationships, obtaining a language that no one in your home community or even your family can understand or use is not a total remedy. Residential schools therefore are communities where the children use their newfound linguistic and consequent social abilities to explore themselves, their peers, and the adult world. In the classroom, deaf students are prepared with language education for learning the tools of our civilization—subjects taught through that very special language. The dormitories are the communities in which deaf children learn how to live. They need language to do both.

Schools for the deaf are also often centers of the culture and social life of the greater deaf community. Employment opportunities at the professional, paraprofessional, and blue-collar levels attract deaf adults and their families. They work in the institution, in related services, or in the infrastructure of small businesses serving the institution. Deaf individuals become part of a cultural whole, with their unique language linking their family, economic, and cultural life as is expected in the hearing world. For many deaf children in residence, the school is an alma mater in the purest sense of the expression. Children may well live most of their lives between ages 6 and 18 at a residential school.

Home visiting varies according to the proximity of a school to its source of students. Today most schools promote routine weekend visiting, and in fact some have a five-day school and residence. But this factor is governed by geography and incidence. A nonurban institution that is the primary resource for a sprawling state may well have the bulk of its students there over all but major holiday weekends, unless the parents can afford transportation for themselves to visit at the school or for their child to come home. Costs aside, the distances and difficulties of commercial transportation preclude independent weekend travel visits for younger deaf children.

This circumstance is familiar to professional child care workers. The reasons for residential care are different, but some of its effects are the same, as are the developmental and social/emotional opportunities that can be taken. The best use of this time depends on the degree of knowledge and professionalism in the staff itself and among supervisors. Too often weekends are viewed merely as downtime, on one hand, or as activity periods to keep idle hands busy, on the other. Neither extreme, regardless of financial expense or saving to institution, affords the quality interpersonal time or therapeutic programming by design that professional child and youth care offers.

THE LANGUAGES

All of us use visual communication. We read, use, and respond to facial expression and body language both consciously and unconsciously. We wave good-bye and nod our heads in agreement, frown or smile, grin or grimace in visual communication. We don't depend on it for detailed information, negotiation, contracting, or obtaining directions when lost in a strange part of town. Though it is a part of every interpersonal communication, it is not the primary means of delivering or obtaining a message. We depend on speech and hearing. We learned to understand and use speech because we could hear. We were not taught to speak in a formal way. We learned by being able to hear conversation in our environment whether it was directed toward us or not. We acquired speech and the meanings of everyday words through the pervasive use and endless repetition of language around us. We could use our expanding vocabulary to ask more about meaning and the unknown and the unfamiliar. Language became a sophisticated tool of our curiosity and our primary identification.

Prelingually deaf children must learn language in a visual form. The visual communication mentioned above is secondary only to the use of speech and hearing. Prelingually deaf children in hearing families depend on this secondary method for all of their communication until or unless the families begin to use a visually coded form of language, or until they reach a school that offers it. Too often, children and families have no systematic primary communication at all during the preschool years when it is so important to adaptive ego development, self-image, informal learning, pace of cognitive development, and emotional security. Deaf children must learn a visual language that possesses the potential for all of the functions of conventional language with a minimum of ambiguity. Schools for the deaf cannot assume that the children arrive with a basic vocabulary comparable to the hearing child or to children with handicaps other than auditory.

The first task is to teach a visual language. Most residential schools use a so-called Total Communication method. Words are pronounced while manual equivalents are presented so that the movements made by lips and face during speech occur simultaneously with sign. Electronic amplification is employed to enhance the use of residual hearing. Speech therapy is employed and speech reading is taught to maximize the use of conventional communication forms to the extent of each child's capacity. Therefore children learning to communicate through Total Communication methods may use voice and lip movement as well as sign as part of their expressive language, and they might depend on those components in their receptive language as well. Others known as "oral schools" focus exclusively and intensively on vocalization, speech reading, and state-of-the-art amplification.

The sign language used in Total Communication is called Manually Coded English, or MCE, in which there is a sign equivalent for each spoken word presented in the same order as standard spoken English. Total Communication uses English syntax in the visual modes of sign and speech-reading, as well as the auditory mode of vocalization.

Finger-spelling is a form of manual communication in which each actual letter in a word is spelled with one hand according to an accepted alphabet. Many finger formations bear a resemblance to the letter being presented. Finger-spelling is rarely used as a primary manual language, but it is often used as an adjunct to a visual language method for precision, specificity, and to identify unfamiliar vocabulary.

While learning about deaf children, this writer was most grateful to deaf child care staff members who were able to show him the economical use of sign that more accurately and graphically described a technical concept than the word itself, spoken or spelled. The writer had finger-spelled "projection" and then proceeded to illustrate laboriously and awkwardly the psychological mechanism of defense projection in idiosyncratic pantomime. An astute staff member recognized the notion and created a sign on the spot. It was a finger-spelled "P" originating at the chest as the center of feeling, then the hand with the "P" was rapidly thrust forward, the arm extended and the index finger pointing toward another person, present or imagined. This clearly was not a projection of future earnings or gross national product. It was psychological projection, and the sign itself contained that connotation. Sign is an exciting and creative language. It is an adventure!

The principal language among those who depend on visual communication is known as American Sign Language, or ASL. In ASL the syntax and idiom are radically different from spoken language. It is the language used within a deaf community, exquisitely expressive and amazingly economical for the deaf person to use in contrast to lipreading, MCE, or finger-spelling. Although many of the signs are the same as those used in MCE, it is not the signs themselves that make the difference. ASL cannot be directly translated to spoken language, as can be done with MCE. Translation requires more than one step of interpretation, as perhaps an English-Chinese dialogue might require in either direction. By way of contrast, English-German or English-Spanish dialogues are more directly translatable despite necessary adjustments of word order. Though there are differences in syntax among spoken languages, and there are always idioms that defy translation, their lack of total equivalence does not approach that of the ASL-MCE or ASL-spoken English language differences. Grammatical structure, strong visual paralinguistic components, and reliance on visual metaphor do not have easily available spoken language equivalents. A deaf person with no language other than ASL will have a problem understanding MCE for the same reasons that a hearing or deaf person who knows MCE exclusively is entirely lost in conversation with an individual using ASL. Fluency in ASL, useful and rich as it is within the deaf community, does not alone infer fluency in MCE or access to written communication. Fortunately, most deaf people become bilingual in both manual languages. They are able to communicate in ASL and MCE. Between these two very different manual languages, intermediate forms are emerging. The deaf have a rich and energetic culture, including their languages.

Within deaf education controversy exists over whether the use of ASL should be encouraged or discouraged, whether it should be formally taught to deaf students, and if so at what level of schooling, and whether it should be used as a language of instruction or not. Be that as it may, ASL is the dominant language used within the deaf community. Residential schools being very much a part of and in some places central to a deaf community, ASL will be found there whether it is in the classroom or not.

The deaf, who must rely totally on their vision for understanding language, and on their manual dexterity, and facial and body movement to express language, expend great concentration and energy to do so. The visual receptive mode alone is more physiologically expensive than the auditory. Eyes can get very tired. Therefore, ASL, with its remarkable syntax, visual metaphor, and conceptual condensation, is the preferred language among the deaf. Manually Coded English is comparatively quite physiologically expensive; it is common for the deaf to complain of how "hearing people use too many words." ASL, however, with its unique syntax, can be extremely difficult for the hearing person to learn. Most hearing persons entering the field of deafness at first learn MCE. The child care worker who brings his professional skills to the deaf school will find that MCE will serve quite well. Although receptive skills are always more difficult to acquire in a second language, the impact of saturation in a dormitory provides the motivation and the opportunity for rapid improvement. Good receptive language skills in the child care worker are imperative for the child's nurturing. In any case, the worker's language skills will achieve greatest improvement on the job. Manual languages are three-dimensional forms of communication in motion that do not lend themselves to solitary or textbook study. The paralinguistics are too important, and the three-dimensional aspect alone requires that the student of any sign language study with people who know that language as well as those who are also learning.

DEAF CHILD—HEARING FAMILY

Deaf children of hearing families are often deprived children. The communication handicap has deprived them of being understood. They are most eager to help their worker understand them. Too often the worker also has had to consciously learn a language. The patience of many of these children with the beginning signer is astounding.

Their need to know and to be known is no less than that for any child. Their need for understanding and nurturing is great. Despite their native intelligence, many are delayed several years in cognitive, social, and emotional development. This is to be expected as a consequence of not having access to a viable communication system until school age. Of course, their handicap has also had a distressful impact on their families.

One of the more difficult and unfortunately common complications for deaf children and their hearing families occurs when the very young child serves as a lightning rod for a distressed household. Child care workers are all too familiar with the severe impact on the psychological maturation of the many children in care who have been blamed since infancy for the problems of their families. These families have severe structural and communicative problems. Children assume the burden and the negative self-image consequent to that role assignment. In care, we find them both overtly and subtly vacillating between being self-deprecating and hopelessly morose, and having severe behavior problems—acting as if any expectation of them were a trap or trick to demonstrate their incompetence and uselessness. In either phase or combination, many of these children are in a psychological and cognitive growth moratorium. Deaf children of hearing families without a language that the child can share are exquisitely sensitive to the unexplored, unexplained, and uninterpreted facial expressions and body language of significant others in their lives. Toddlers in their phase-appropriate egocentricity may well begin to assume emotional and behavioral blame for any distress they feel among their loved ones, and they can subtly learn that the toddler is available for scapegoating. Family problems of any kind can promote this kind of distortion of a child's role. A hearing family with a deaf child is at very high risk for this unconscious misuse of their child, and the child's confirmation of such a role.

Many deaf children have undergone severe damage to their self-images and see themselves in grossly negative terms. Many, unfortunately, have learned at home or in community preschool and elementary school experiences that they are able to obtain negative attention at will by their own efforts. They view positive attention as randomized and not a consequence of their own behavior. Time and time again, experience shapes their negative behavior and confirms the self-image that goes with it. Since attention is an objective, and negative attention has proven predictable, they aim at the predictable.

Child care workers are familiar with these patterns and have learned through experience how to work with them. The body of knowledge of child and youth care is needed to help in the task of enabling deaf children to find their way through the social and emotional consequences of their deafness, and the delay in realizing their cognitive potential. The issue does not dwell in undoing deafness or in creating hearing children out of deaf children. It centers on providing a climate of constancy of person, consistency of nurturing and an ability to apply the body of knowledge of child and youth care tailored to each child's need to grow.

Prelingually deaf children of hearing families are likely to be delayed in many areas of development. These children can best catch up when they acquire language in an intimate and nurturing climate. They can proceed through the normal order of developmental phases, albeit with some lag. Recognition of these phases, their necessity, and their process is a knowledge base central to child care. Providing the circumstances in which growth experiences can occur and stimulating those experiences is a task of child care. An apparently ordinary event at a traditional residential school provides an illustration of the need for knowledgeable child care in that setting. Some years ago I was offering a miniseminar in child development to dormitory staff members. After a session on the preschool years, when dramatic play requiring communication, negotiation, and collaboration among children is common, I was approached by one of the housemothers, who guided me carefully to an obscure corner to chat quietly. She needed to be sure that we would not be overheard, and that our conversation would not be visible to her deaf colleagues, who she feared might read our lips. She needed confidentiality.

After school, her 25 boys, six to nine years of age, return to the dormitory, change clothes, and then are expected to remain in the playground outside of the dorm building until time to prepare for the evening meal. Her job is to ensure that all of the children are there, and that no one gets hurt. In the playground are swings, seesaws, slides, and a fair amount of space in which to run. All of the equipment invites solitary or parallel play, associative at best. The only rule needed to use the equipment is to patiently take turns. The child who cannot not do that well might play "chase" or gravitate to sandbox play in the dirt by the bushes. All of these activities are acceptable so long as all of the children are in sight of the staff person and no one gets hurt.

A problem had developed recently. She noticed four boys missing during one of the nose counts, although the proper number were present at a second count after returning indoors. At the time, she was unable to identify who had been missing, and on the correct recount forgot the matter. Keeping precise track of over 20 active little boys under any circumstances is difficult. Since deaf youngsters require line of sight for communication with the staff, it is a more than absorbing task. The following day she did notice some boys leaving the playground to sneak back into the building.

On the third day, she had arranged for a relief person to stay outside with the children while she searched through the building for the missing ones. She discovered that the children were very busy. They had rearranged the furniture in their army barracks dormitory into a kind of enclosure. Within, the boys were actively talking with each other. They didn't notice her watching through the doorway because their visual attention was devoted to the negotiation of who would play what role and how in a game of "house." There had to be a father, mother, baby, and another person.

At first this writer assumed that the housemother's distress was because the boys were indoors instead of outside where expected and observable, but she was too upset for so simple an assumption. She felt that she ought to stop the boys and scold them. She had stopped herself because she feared that doing so would be harmful. She was concerned about the boys playing house in general and crossing gender roles in particular. She felt that they were too old to be playing house and their need to do this suggested that they had homosexual tendencies. Her usual behavior would have been to interrupt and send them back outside with a scolding about sneaking off. She would not have addressed the homosexual issue with them or with anyone else in the school because of embarrassment in just talking about it, if for no other reason.

The coincidence of the miniseminar and the boys' play created enough useful doubt for her to have watched them play and then go back outside to worry. She confessed that she was concerned about possibly hurting the children by intruding but did not know what she could do in good conscience. In the course of conversation, and using the seminar as a point of reference, she was able to accept that the boys were demonstrating exactly the kind of developmental behavior that we had been talking about. It was in phase but delayed. The recognition that deaf youngsters are more immature in general than their hearing agemates was generally acceptable. The specifics were more troublesome to accept. Indeed, these boys were using language exactly as it should be used given their place in the sequence of developmental phases. By making the opportunity for themselves to negotiate dramatic play, they were telling us what they needed, beyond the slides and swings of the playground. Perhaps they had sensed the probability of peer or adult disapproval. One or more may have been scolded at home or in the community for baby play. Perhaps they sought privacy from the chaos of the chasing games. Perhaps they sought the props that the dorm might provide.

As it turned out, the housemother was able to accept the assurance that the dramatic play was phase appropriate, that the content was a natural early scenario of children as they reach that phase, and that it was not a signal of perversion. The next time she was able to join them, she invited them outside where she had found a place out of the line of chase where they would play peacefully. She chided them about having sneaked into the dorm without permission. Soon the school was able to provide an outdoor playhouse so that dramatic play could be openly endorsed and encouraged. In this instance, the play was not regressive but progressive.

Too often, children in institutions, whatever the reason, do not have the opportunity to follow the natural developmental progression of their psychological growth, especially when that growth has been delayed. Too often, children of eight and nine are expected to participate in competitive-collaborative games such as softball, before they have been able to move out of the solitary or parallel play of the toddler in the sandbox. The expectation ignores the intermediate rule-making stage of dramatic play when children conform to behavior that is negotiated with their playmates.

Sometimes the imposition of structured games such as softball by an enthusiastic recreation staff has resulted in a war between the children and the staff members, who find themselves forced to make the children play ball while the outfielder drifts off to the bushes and plays in the sand and the third baseman, with or without language, sees no reason whatsoever to try to catch the ball and tag someone, except that he will be praised for doing so or punished for not doing so. The programming and cognitive leap from sliding board to organized sport is simply too great. The more active children rebel, the more passive ones attempt conformity. Neither group learns the game, and both are impressed again with how adults try to make them do things the children do not understand, and in fact are not ready to understand.

PROFESSIONAL POSSIBILITIES IN DEAF CHILD CARE

For many years residential schools for the deaf selected dormitory staff members who were able to sign or were willing to learn on their own. The choice emphasized language skills while child care considerations were ignored or unidentified beyond the extremes of "being kind" or being able to discipline. Child care was viewed as incidental to the academic task, and professional child care was unknown. As deaf residential school populations are becoming smaller, the schools have begun to act on the recognition that child care can enhance academic achievement and vocational adjustment among the children in their programs. They welcome the opportunity to expand the adaptive capacities of deaf students in social and emotional maturation through quality child care.

Moreover, the multihandicapped deaf child population is being identified with many subcategories of combinations of handicapping conditions. The schools are discovering an increasing demand for specialized and knowledgeable therapeutic child care in serving these populations.

Direct collaboration among child care workers, teachers, parents, and clinical resource staff members is necessary to find and use every bit of pertinent information, which is often obscured by the childrens' linguistic and other problems. It takes concentration, self-discipline, thoughtfulness, and sensitivity to glean these data from them. The individual child's program requires tailoring and integration of the academic and the child care tasks as part of the same mission. This is in contrast to the traditional structures in many schools where the dormitory staff had little contact with the academic and support staff either as sources or recipients of information. The vertical administrative structures that serve accountability but not a developmental database for planning for individual children, are giving way to horizontal arrangements that at least encourage and often require active communication at the frontline level of the child's living and learning experience. The need to fine-tune the steps in stimulating growth, development, and learning for each child has generated changes that require the staff to be educated in the body of knowledge of child care and its applications to special populations. More schools are willing to invest in providing intensive language training and technical information about deafness to professional child and youth care workers interested in exploring child care with the deaf.

Deaf children suffer at least as much from child abuse, mental illness, learning disabilities, and family problems, with attendant behavior problems, as the child population at large. Indeed, the prevalence may be greater. Quite recently an additional form of care has appeared. In a few places, alternative group care for deaf children who cannot be managed in a traditional school dormitory is being developed. Therapeutic group care agencies, where the use of child care expertise is standard practice, and where it has been the traditional focus of the center, have become interested in work with the deaf. They are developing cottages on their grounds and group homes in the community through collaboration with local schools and agencies that serve deaf children. As is true for hearing children, the group residence is an entity of its own devoted to the primary mission of providing therapeutic care to children who are severely emotionally and socially disturbed. These children happen to be deaf as well.

In this model, intensive language training for the staff is a requirement, as is the employment of deaf staff members who can become educated in professional child care work. A value of this model is that the agency views itself as being primarily in a therapeutic role. A small deaf school may not be able to devote its resources to developing the therapeutic role parallel to its academic role for an exceptional minority of its enrollment; but it may be able to provide active consultation and financial and classroom support to a residential center or group home. Both agencies could pool recreational programming. There might be a kind of mainstreaming to the benefit of both hearing and deaf children and the staffs of the deaf school and the child care agency.

Another area of interest currently emerging is the need for small community-based group homes or halfway houses for young adults who are deaf and have other handicaps that interfere with their social and economic adaptability.

Many of these young people were damaged by the rubella epidemic over 20 years ago. Their social and economic habilitation is taking the form of special programs in the community similar to and sometimes combined with those for handicapped hearing young adults. The homes, often called transitional youth programs, are oriented toward experiential learning of independent-living and working skills. Much of the knowledge and technique of professional child care is directly applicable to the guidance, modeling, and support that the staff members of the homes require. Professional child care workers are becoming interested in serving transitional youth. There are young deaf adults among them.

SUMMARY

A long overdue trend toward more specialized and quality child care for the deaf is taking place. It is occurring within the traditional schools as they actively search for professional child care staff members and the new forms of administration to best use them. It is occurring among community child care agencies and the independent-living centers, as described above. All are searching for ways to apply effectively the best of both fields to the needs of deaf children and youths. Though the population of deaf children is relatively small, the variety of specialized care required is great. The use of many different models of care can serve to complement each other in providing for the array. In work with the deaf, child and youth care professionals will find more than the usual opportunities for advancement, plenty of professional stimulation, challenge, and need for creative application of their skills.

SELECTED RESOURCES

Brill, R., MacNeil, B. and Newman, L. 1986. Framework for appropriate programs for deaf children. In *1986 Reference Issue, American Annals of the Deaf*, ed. W.N. Craig and W.B. Craig, 131 (2): 65–77.

A child care worker with an interest in deafness will find the Annals reference issue a major resource for the United States and Canada. It lists schools by state and province, and has a tabular summary of statistics for the United States. It also lists professional training programs, social clubs for the deaf, research and demonstration projects, and professional organizations. There are readable and informative articles on appropriate programs for the deaf; the necessity for residential schools' services to multihandicapped, sensory-impaired children; and a comparison of data on hearing-impaired children under age six in surveys of 1977 and 1984.

Naiman, D.W. ed. 1972. *Inservice training for after class staff in residential schools, deafness research and training center.* New York: New York University.

———. ed. 1973. *Handbook for staff development in residential schools for deaf children, deafness research and training center.* New York: New York University.

Both of Naiman's publications illustrate the effort of the deaf education leadership over a decade ago to find ways to improve the child care aspect of their responsibilities. The Handbook describes the efforts of six deaf schools in staff development and contains a guide for inservice programs.

Schlesinger, H., and Meadow, K.P., 1972. *Sound and Sign.* Berkeley, CA: University of California Press.

The authors present a thorough, sensitive, and well-researched picture of mental health issues and childhood deafness. Their use of E.H. Erikson's developmental model, familiar to professional child care workers, as applied to problems of deafness, is unexcelled.

VI

The Involvement of Family Members as Consumers in Treatment Programs for Troubled Youths

Thom Garfat

THE MOTHER WITH THE GUITAR

Barbara was a 15-year-old Native Canadian girl admitted to the residential treatment center because of community and behavior problems. She lived in the girls' unit with nine other youngsters of various cultural and ethnic backgrounds.

Barbara's relationship with her family was characterized by alienation and isolation. She rejected the values and attitudes of her parents, extended family, and community, and particularly rejected her mother and the things that her mother believed in.

As part of the regular unit program, family members spent time visiting with their children and were involved in ways in which they had something to contribute to the group. Barbara's mother showed a desire to be involved. She played guitar very well and liked to sing many of the old, and some of the more contemporary, western tunes. As her way of participating in the program, she came regularly to the unit, and played her guitar and sang for those youngsters who were interested.

Barbara was angry that her mother wanted to be involved in this way. She saw her mother's guitar playing and singing as representative of the cultures and values that she wanted so desperately to reject. In spite of Barbara's objections, her mother continued.

At first when the mother came to play and sing, only a few girls would sit with her to listen or learn. Barbara would involve herself in some other activity. Over time, more of the girls in the program gathered around, and some of them began to show an interest in learning to play the guitar so that they too might sing songs that reflected stages of sadness, aloneness, or worry. The unit purchased a few guitars so that the girls could practice in between Barbara's mother's visits.

As this activity began to evolve around her mother, Barbara increasingly heard comments from other youngsters about how they liked or appreciated her mother. Invariably these comments made Barbara angry, and she acted out even more.

Soon the Tuesday evenings with Barbara's mother, the guitars, and the western songs became a regular feature of the unit program. It was not mandatory, but because they were learning a new way to express themselves, many of the youngsters chose to participate. As more youngsters participated, more staff members participated as well, and they began to ask Barbara's mother if she knew other songs that were derived more directly from her own culture. Barbara's mother sang some of them for the group. From this expression of culture in a learning and sharing context came a greater sensitivity to and awareness of the values, beliefs, and attitudes of the mother's group of Native Canadians.

Over time, Barbara was able to see her mother somewhat differently. She eventually approached her mother to learn how to play the guitar and how to sing some of the songs that the other youngsters seemed to enjoy so much. She found pride in her history and culture, and other children found a new way of seeing culture and cultural identity. Some of them then developed an interest in their own backgrounds and histories.

The staff members also realized that they needed to become more familiar with the cultures of the other children. Through the use of music they began to help other children explore their own culture and its uniqueness. Barbara's mother also helped the agency to realize that it needed to be more sensitive to the cultures from which children come.

Barbara and her mother did not live happily ever after but

through this experience Barbara found a way to value and appreciate her mother as a person. They found a way to share an enjoyable experience, and now one sometimes finds them together singing and playing new songs or learning old ones from each other.

BACKGROUND

Available literature, research, and program models clearly suggest that treatment programs for children and youths are enhanced by family involvement in a variety of program areas [Brendtro and Ness 1985; Taylor and Alpert 1982; Whittaker 1981, 1985]. In many Canadian provinces this move is supported by laws regarding the rights of children and families to be involved (see the Youth Protection Act of Quebec [updated July 1984] and the Young Offenders Act of Canada [1984]).

The evolution and development of family systems therapy has done much to promote family involvement, because it has demonstrated the benefits that result from an encompassing systemic approach to the treatment of childrens' disturbances. From involvement in family therapy, it has been only a short step to involvement in other ways such as serving on the board of directors or taking part in a special outing.

The involvement of young people and their families in a treatment program, however, cannot be approached in a random fashion. Without an understanding of the possible impacts of involvement, child and youth care professionals are unable to predict or prepare for this change. General systems thinking provides us with a way to understand the involvement of family members and helps us to better understand some of the potential outcomes. The purpose of this chapter is to provide a systemic framework for organizing our thinking about the involvement of children and families, as consumers, in child and youth care agencies. With this framework it will be possible for agency personnel to make decisions about where, when and how to involve consumers.

WHO ARE THE CONSUMERS?

Anyone who has involvement with the treatment agency is a consumer on one level or another. Globally, society is the ultimate consumer of child and youth care services because agencies provide a resource for dealing with some of society's most troubled members. It is irrelevant whether the intent of society is to provide treatment services for troubled young people or to use treatment programs as a way to remove less desirable members from its midst [Fewster and Garfat 1987]. The fact remains that society consumes the services of child and youth care agencies for some of its members.

More directly, the social service community is also a consumer of agency services. The people that identify the needs, refer the young people, or supply support services are all consumers of our services. They use our services with the expectation that some specific outcome will occur and will be either satisfied or dissatisfied with the results.

Most intimately and intensely, the most directly affected consumers are the young people and families who are directly involved (parents, siblings, and extended family). They are the principal focus of this chapter. The framework presented, however, will serve as a guide for the involvement of other consumers as well.

WHY INVOLVE FAMILY MEMBERS?

The literature [Brendtro and Ness 1985; Fewster and Garfat 1987] suggests that family involvement is here to stay. Despite the potential difficulties in undergoing the necessary role differentiation between various treatment staff members (e.g., social workers and child and youth care workers) and the changing of attitudes to see "parents as partners" [Brendtro and Ness 1985; Whittaker 1985], there is a general consensus that the inclusion of family members in treatment agencies has beneficial long-term results.

Family members bring with them the values and attitudes of the culture and community from which their child has been removed. Child and youth care professionals frequently work in isolation from these values and attitudes and can benefit from the continuity that is established when they are incorporated into treatment programs. The continuity of understanding and experience also provides a greater ease of transition for the child from the treatment program back into the community. The more that child and youth care professionals are aware of, sensitive to, and involved with the culture and community of the young persons in care, the more effective they will be.

Parents bring with them years of previous experience with their child and can help child and youth care professionals understand what does, or does not, work. Their insights about needs, behaviors, and psychodynamics can be extremely helpful to program staff members who are just getting to know a child. Maintaining regular relationships with family members also helps young people in care feel less separated and isolated from their roots. With the regular involvement of his or her family, a young person is likely to feel more helped than rejected, and discharge will be less traumatic. Placement becomes an experience shared by the family, rather than an experience that just happened to one of its members.

The involvement of family members in the treatment process (or agency) also helps signal that problems are family-based, and counteracts the message that the problem lies only in the young person. Including family members suggests to them that they have an important role to play in the helping process. Because of their involvement they may see themselves as resources, rather than as failures or causes of problems. It also allows the treatment staff to see families in this new light [Sonnenschein 1981], and supports a change in attitude among child and youth care professionals.

Family members also have unique resources. Like members of the agency (frontline workers, supervisors, social workers, administrators, support persons, and members of the board), they have attitudes, beliefs, expectations, values, feelings, knowledge, and skills that can have a positive influence on the daily treatment environment.

THE TREATMENT ORGANIZATION AS A SYSTEM

Systems theory provides us with a way of understanding the context within which family involvement can occur. Berrien (1968) provided us with a simple, yet graphic, way of thinking of organizations as systems, and his thinking has been adapted to social service agencies by writers like Lauffer (1985). Figure 1 shows how every part of the system is connected to every other part. (Items in the boxes are examples only, and do not represent everything that is actually involved.)

To speak of an agency as a system is to speak of all the parts of the organization that interact with each other, either directly or indirectly. Because any part of the system interacts with, is affected by, and affects every other part of the system, a change in any part will provoke a change in some other part, which will, in

Figure 1. The Treatment Organization as a System (Adapted from Berrien, 1969)

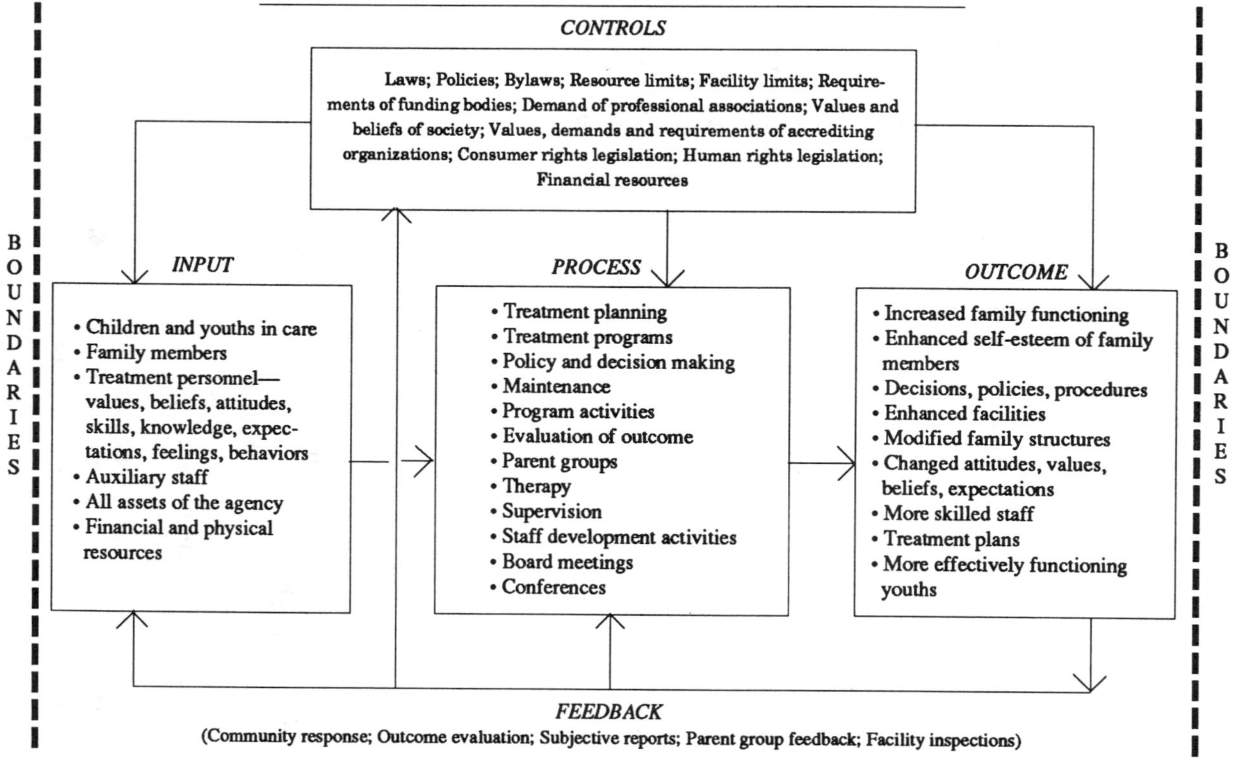

BOUNDARIES

CONTROLS

Laws; Policies; Bylaws; Resource limits; Facility limits; Requirements of funding bodies; Demand of professional associations; Values and beliefs of society; Values, demands and requirements of accrediting organizations; Consumer rights legislation; Human rights legislation; Financial resources

INPUT

- Children and youths in care
- Family members
- Treatment personnel—values, beliefs, attitudes, skills, knowledge, expectations, feelings, behaviors
- Auxiliary staff
- All assets of the agency
- Financial and physical resources

PROCESS

- Treatment planning
- Treatment programs
- Policy and decision making
- Maintenance
- Program activities
- Evaluation of outcome
- Parent groups
- Therapy
- Supervision
- Staff development activities
- Board meetings
- Conferences

OUTCOME

- Increased family functioning
- Enhanced self-esteem of family members
- Decisions, policies, procedures
- Enhanced facilities
- Modified family structures
- Changed attitudes, values, beliefs, expectations
- More skilled staff
- Treatment plans
- More effectively functioning youths

FEEDBACK

(Community response; Outcome evaluation; Subjective reports; Parent group feedback; Facility inspections)

BOUNDARIES

turn, provoke change in another part in an infinite series of changes. Thus, in systems theory, the statement is made that a change in any part of the system brings about a change in the total system; all parts of a system are related in this way.

Figure 1 presents the treatment organization as an interrelated system, and represents how all parts of a system can be categorized. It helps us understand the agency in a more orderly fashion so that we can consider the areas in which we may want consumer involvement. Each box of the diagram represents a subsystem within the larger system.

The *Controls* subsystem includes anything that limits the functioning of the system. Controls may originate from outside the system (e.g., laws, the values of society, or the requirements of funding bodies) or they may come from inside (e.g., agency policies). Whether generated externally or internally, controls establish parameters or limits of acceptable functioning for the agency.

It may be, for example, that the board of directors has established a policy that parents must have a copy of their child's treatment plan. One result of this policy may be a practice that treatment plans must be written in a language that parents, as lay persons, can understand. This, then, places a limit on what is acceptable as a treatment plan within a program. In this way, information from the controls subsystem affects the language used (input), the treatment intervention (process), and the outcome (parents are more informed).

The *Input* subsystem includes everything that is a resource for the processes of the system—everything available to do the jobs that must be done. In general, inputs include all the characteristics of the people involved in the agency (staff members or consumers), the financial and physical resources available, and the overall environment of the agency. Resources may be determined by the controls subsystem, as in the case of a law that requires that all child and youth care workers be certified, or a regulation that the physical plant must provide a specific number of square feet per child. They also include the individual values, beliefs, knowledge, and skills of all the people involved

The *Process* subsystem includes all the activities that occur in the agency: treatment activities, maintenance activities, meetings, conferences, program activities, supervision, and any other activity that might take place. Processes are affected by the controls subsystem, which may dictate that some activities must take place take place (e.g., a policy that all workers have the right to regular supervision), and by input, which determines the resources available to carry out the activities (e.g., the supervisor's skills).

It may be, for example, that the senior managers decide on a policy (control) that all child and youth care workers must receive training (process) in the area of managing aggressive children (process) and therefore employs only supervisors (input) who have appropriate knowledge (input). It is clear that the processes of the agency are affected by both the controls and input subsystems.

The *Outcome* subsystem includes all the products of the processes of the system. For every process or activity there will be an outcome. The outcome of the treatment process may be families and children who are better able to cope; the outcome of maintenance activities may be a more attractive physical environment; and the outcome of staff training may be child and youth care workers who are more effective and who think of themselves as professionals.

Negative outcomes are also possible. Ineffective supervision might lead to ineffective child care workers, which might in turn lead to ineffective treatment. Additionally, outcomes can be direct, as in the case above, or they can be indirect, such as the feelings of failure staff members might have when treatment outcomes are less than desired. Anything that results from an activity within the agency is an outcome.

Feedback in a system refers to any information provided to the system that allows it to evaluate itself and its potential need for change. It may include, for example, formal data such as measures of treatment effectiveness, evaluations of the physical facility, or surveys about supervisory satisfaction. It may also include more informal information, such as staff absences, letters from families, and community responses to the program.

As seen in figure 1, feedback can flow from any subsystem to any other. For example, if families say that they feel rejected, that feedback may go directly to the board of directors (control) or to the treatment personnel (input). Depending on the response, the feedback may or may not promote a change that would affect the process subsystem in regards to family involvement.

If the feedback went directly to the board, it could set a new policy that families must be included in treatment programming. This new policy may now demand that staff training (process) include knowledge and skills for effective family involvement, which might influence treatment outcomes and the feelings of families during and after treatment. Subsequent outcome information will then inform the system (via the feedback loop) about the effectiveness of the new policy.

The *Boundaries* of a system can be thought of as the system's limits, which show up as the rules about who participates and how they participate, within the system [Minuchin 1974].

All systems and subsystems have boundaries. When the system is closed to information from outside itself, we say the boundaries are rigid. When the system is appropriately open to information from outside itself, we say the boundaries are clear. When the system is overreactive to information, the boundaries are diffuse. Figure 2 represents the continuum of rigidity or diffuseness of boundaries that may exist in a system, whether that system is an agency, a child and youth care program, or a family.

The clarity or diffuseness of the boundaries is indicated by the degree of reactivity the system shows to information from outside itself. For example, if evidence is presented to a team that including families makes it easier for residents to move home and the team rejects that information without consideration, the boundaries can be said to be more rigid. If the team, without adequate consideration, immediately includes all family members in all aspects of the program, the boundaries are more diffuse.

In a system with clear boundaries, the information can be considered and evaluated according to program goals, and a decision can be made regarding how, where, and to what degree families should be included, depending on the desired outcome. The boundaries will form the rules about how and where family members are to be included.

The foregoing has shown how all parts of the agency system are connected and how a change in one part can influence other parts. The following example may illustrate the statement made at the beginning of this section that a change in any one part of the system will promote a change in the whole system.

> A residential treatment program operated under a traditional system of excluding family members from their program. Parents were informed of their child's progress on a regular basis but were never actively involved, with the exception of regular sessions with the unit therapist.
>
> One of the child care workers attended a workshop on getting family members involved in residential programs

Figure 2. Boundaries [Adapted from Minuchin (1974)]

RIGID	*CLEAR*	*DIFFUSE*
little reactivity	*appropriate reactivity*	*extreme reactivity*

and came away with the belief that her unit could benefit from more family involvement.

At the next team meeting she presented the idea and while the others were initially nervous, the team agreed to invite a fairly cooperative family of a resident boy to spend an evening in the program during the next week. From that one evening visit the following resulted:

- The family members felt more involved and asked to come back another time.
- The team understood the boy better and made changes in the treatment plan.
- The boy felt that the staff cared more and talked to them about his family.
- Because the boy talked more to the staff members they were able to help him leave sooner.
- The staff members wondered if maybe involving families of other children would help as well, so they invited several more, not always with the same result.
- Team members who were tired found their team meetings more animated and enjoyable.
- They enjoyed new challenges and this affected the atmosphere of the unit.
- They decided to fix up one of the rooms so that children could meet with their families in private and requested some paint from the maintenance department.
- The maintenance department reported the request to the agency director, who decided to find out what was going on. She liked what she saw and told the staff.

- The staff appreciated the positive feedback; they seldom got it, and they started to feel special and important again.
- The changes continued and are still continuing. At last report the treatment team and the families were making a presentation to the board of directors about a proposed change in policy to involve family members in other processes of the agency. This change in policy will create new input for the staff training program, change the hiring practices for new staff members and eventually change the agency's position in the community, all because one worker came back to the unit with a new idea for including family members.

Although this example presents a positive change in a system, all changes may not necessarily have the same positive effect. Any move by an agency or program to change its system by involving consumers must be taken with care and consideration.

Before addressing the questions of where, when, and how to involve families, we must recognize that every system is both contained by, and composed of, other systems. It is to the idea of systems within systems that the next section of this chapter is addressed. We will then be ready to look at possible roles for family members in the agency.

SYSTEMS WITHIN SYSTEMS

All things occur in context. All systems are subsystems of larger systems. The process of treatment, within the larger agency system, represents a subsystem within a system. Figure 3 represents this concept.

We find within one system (e.g., the treatment process system) yet another subsystem, in an infinite regression down to the point where the simplest interaction between any members of the team can also be seen as a system.

Thinking of treatment processes as subsystems within systems helps us realize that the controls, inputs, processes, outcome, and feedback of the larger organization have an impact on the smallest of subsystems functioning within the organization, and that changes in the smallest system will affect the larger system.

Figure 3. Systems Within Systems

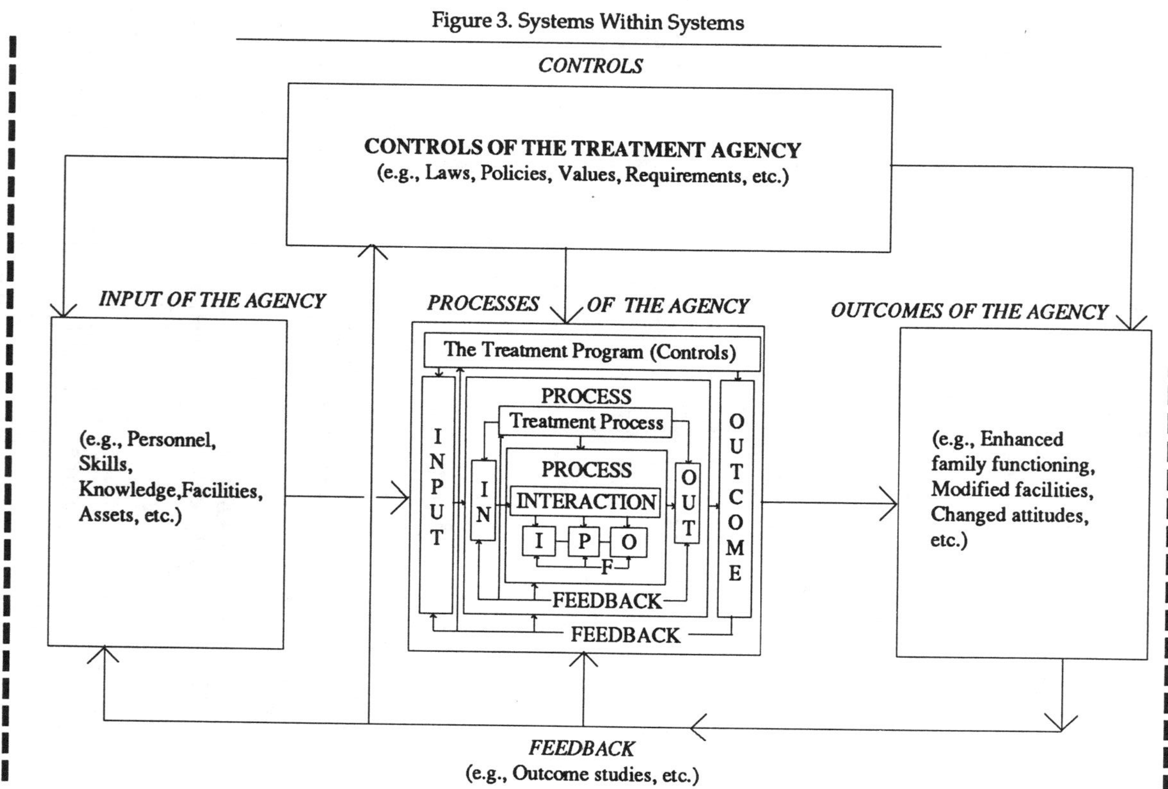

The earlier example demonstrates how a change in the treatment program subsystem can affect the rest of the system. Familiarity with the concepts can be enhanced by speculating on any possible change within the system as described, and following the outcome of that change through the larger system. This makes it easier to see how input affects change, and that change, through the feedback process, effects more change.

In systems terms, this represents the concept of an open system (as opposed to a closed system). It is available to accept new information. The goal is to develop agencies that are open to the involvement of consumers and to develop subsystems within the treatment agency that also have clear boundaries for consumer involvement.

POSSIBLE ROLES FOR FAMILY MEMBERS WITHIN THE TREATMENT ORGANIZATION

Once one is thinking systemically one can consider possible roles for family members. The following ideas are offered as stimulus for thought.

Controls

Family members can be involved as active voting members of the board of directors of an agency-system. As consumers of services they can bring a unique inside perspective of the agency, which makes them excellent critics of proposed changes. Consumers can also be involved in policy-making committees, the establishment of procedures, and program development. They can help set guidelines for parent groups and serve as a liaison between the board and other families involved in programs.

Within the treatment program itself, family members can be involved in determining policies, rules, or program activities. Child and youth care workers can invite them to review proposed program changes or to be part of establishing annual program goals.

In the treatment process families and youths can be involved in determining treatment goals, strategies, and frequency and location of family meetings. By supporting the families in these areas, child and youth care professionals facilitate change in families' perceptions of treatment.

Input

The primary input role for family members is as participants in the treatment process. Their skills, attitudes, values, expectations, behaviors, feelings, and knowledge are also valuable in other ways. In other words, a family member who is a professional landscaper can help design changes for the agency's grounds. The parent who is a guitar player can help with the planning of a talent evening. Siblings can help plan games and recreational activities. Their involvement is limited only by our imagination.

Processes

Many North American treatment agencies [Brendtro and Ness 1985; Whittaker 1979, 1981] are including family members directly in the general treatment program. In addition to participating in their own therapy, they may also serve as volunteers, as helpers, and as sources of support for treatment personnel. Some programs identify, at the time of intake, particular activities in which individual members can be involved. One family member may be teaching cooking, another giving art lessons, another helping with facility repairs, and yet another reading stories to children in the evening.

Families can also be involved in other decision-making processes and activities such as fund-raising, increasing community awareness, and encouraging other parents to become involved. They can be involved in parent groups, children's groups, multifamily therapy, Christmas parties, weekend outings, and a number of other activities.

Outcomes

Some possible outcomes of family involvement include modified family structures; changed perceptions about themselves and their roles, rights, and obligations in the world; changed attitudes toward problems and disturbances within the community; increased resources to other troubled families; and a greater sense of acceptance in the community at large. Other outcomes include an array of changes in the program itself as it becomes more sensitive to (and relevant for) the needs of family members. As a result, they may become more active and participatory members of the communities in which they live.

Thus, the treatment agency, as a subsystem of the larger

community, contributes to the enhancement of community life by helping it develop new human resources in people who were previously considered to be consumers of, but not contributors to, the community's assets.

Feedback

Families can be involved in program evaluation. They can give feedback on what the environment seems to say, what the meals are like, or what feelings they have when they enter the unit. Team members can seek feedback from family members about whether their language is clear enough, how they approach family members, and whether the latter feel welcomed.

Families' direct feedback can be used to monitor and enhance their own therapy. They can review treatment goals and strategies and participate in team meetings, case conferences, or discharge interviews. They can provide information on how the treatment process can be more inviting; who should be included; and how the family worker can be more helpful. Information can be solicited on virtually all aspects of the program.

Workers also can look for nonverbal feedback. Family members who never show up for unit activities may be saying that they find the program threatening or uninviting. Little children who cry when the family visits may be saying that they find the unit scary. Parents who are unable to set goals in the treatment process may be saying that they experience nonsupport or intimidation.

To keep a system functioning openly and effectively, feedback must constantly be sought, analyzed, and responded to; otherwise the program will become a static rather than a dynamic entity.

DECIDING HOW TO INVOLVE CONSUMERS IN THE TREATMENT ORGANIZATION

Having decided to include consumers, the question really is, "Where does one begin?" Consideration must be given to the potential impact of consumer involvement on the agency. The *first step* is to determine what specific outcomes the agency wants to attain within the various subsystems. Members of the agency may believe, for example, that treatment will improve with greater continuity of relationships between youths and their family members, and might decide to include family members in the program for that reason. Or they may decide that they need more information about the social values and beliefs of the community to which youths are being discharged. This might lead to inviting family members to sit on the board of directors, or developing a parents' association to discuss and share community norms.

The *second step* is to decide which consumers the agency wants to involve. Different family members bring different inputs to the organization. For example, youths in care bring the experience of being in care and parents bring the experience of having a youth in care. If the agency wishes to enhance the experience for the youths, it may decide to involve them in program committees or develop a youths-in-care group. If the agency wants to improve the experience for parents, it may create a parents' committee to discuss ways in which the experience could be better.

All family members do not have the ability to participate in all areas. If we wish to facilitate success experiences for family members, then child and youth care professionals must help them discover the kinds of involvement in which they might be the most successful.

The *third step* is to validate the consumers' role in the agency. We could include consumers in an agency and give them roles that have only token meaning. For example, it would be possible to create a parents' committee but fail to support its formation and functioning or constantly ignore its recommendations. Thus, on paper, the parents' committee would exist, but it would have difficulty in becoming organized or effective.

Validation will occur through the development of policies or practices that ensure consumer involvement and the allocation of the necessary resources. Some organizations have committed themselves to consumer involvement but ensured noninvolvement through failing to validate participation. Programs must be careful not to sabotage family members' involvement through such subtle methods as inviting family members to participate in program activities scheduled at inconvenient times, or by giving family members responsibilities beyond their capability.

> In one poor attempt to allow a girl to represent the youths in a program, she was scheduled for 15 minutes at the end of a staff meeting and then kept waiting for half an hour before being invited into a tense room of tired workers who were anxious to leave. The staff members were nonattentive and the girl was intimidated. When she offered a

criticism of the program, the meeting quickly degenerated into a shouting match. The meeting "proved" to the team that troubled youths were incapable of providing effective input and feedback.

The *fourth step* is to define the roles of consumers and staff members and make explicit the parameters for involvement. Without this clarity both will be frustrated by not knowing what is expected of them. For example, if the role of consumers is to participate in evaluation, it must be clear that they have the power of recommendation but not implementation. They have an input but not a decision-making function. It is also important that each team member has the same expectation as the others. Energy spent on reaching this clarity at the beginning will pay rewards in the end.

The *fifth step* is to ensure that adequate preparation is made for consumer involvement. In the case of involving family members in program activities this means that the agency ensures that staff members understand and accept the reasons for consumer involvement; that they have the skills necessary to support consumers; that the implications of such involvement have been explored; and that the staff members have a welcoming attitude. If board members decide on consumer involvement without staff support, for example, the plan will fail.

If, however, the child and youth care team members want to have consumers involved in their program, they must get the support of senior agency personnel so as to avoid having family members caught between conflicting subsystems of the agency. Troubled families have enough problems of their own without getting involved in the conflicts of agency personnel.

The *sixth step* is to outline the implementation of consumer involvement so that it proceeds in clearly outlined stages. For example, if the agency has decided to involve youths in the evaluation of programs, it may be necessary to first discuss it with staff members; then with the youths; then help the staff to see the youths as a resource; then help the youths understand their new role; then train them in how program evaluation works; then have them meet the program evaluation committee; and so on. Beginning without clear steps contributes to confusion along the way.

The *seventh step* is to determine when and how involvement is to be evaluated. Indicators of successful involvement should be clearly articulated in advance so that success can be measured objectively. By using the systems model, it is possible to generate a number of possible outcomes that may result from such involvement, and all possible outcomes should be considered as areas for evaluation.

It is important that everyone be in agreement before the process begins. Everyone involved should have the opportunity to ask for clarification about the indicators, and discussion should be encouraged before deciding which outcomes and methods of evaluation are most desired.

The *final step* is to determine what the agency is going to do with the evaluation information. Too often, exciting projects have been undertaken with positive and useful outcomes only to have the idea fall to the wayside after the experimental stage because a team or an agency had not decided, in advance, what to do with the results. Having this commitment in advance helps to ensure the continuation of successful program innovations in the future.

CONCLUSION

The decision to include consumers in a treatment program is a complex and potentially overwhelming decision. By considering the agency or program as a system, it is possible to approach the involvement from a planned point of view, allowing members of an agency to control their own development in this vital new area. Through understanding the possible implications of involvement, the agency is able to begin with an attitude of excitement and enthusiasm. For consumers themselves, it marks their transition from the role of treatment problem to the role of treatment resource. The community and the treatment agency then move one step closer to being resources for each other, and we all take one more step toward enhancing the quality of services that troubled young people and their families both need and deserve.

REFERENCES

Berrien, F.K. 1968. A general systems approach to social taxonomy. In *people, groups and organizations*, ed. B. Indik and F.K. Berrien, 110–127.

Brendtro, L.K., and Ness, A.E. 1983. *Re-educating troubled youth: Environments for teaching and treatment*. New York: Aldine Publishing Company.

Fewster, G., and Garfat, T. 1987. Residential child care. In *Professional child and youth care,* ed. C. Derholm et al. Vancouver, BC: University of British Columbia Press.

Garfat, T. 1981. Avoiding success and ensuring failure in working with unmotivated families. *Journal of Child Care* 1 (2).

Lauffer, A. 1985. Understanding your social agency. In *Sage human services guide*, vol. 3. Beverly Hills, CA: Sage Publishing.

Minuchin, S. 1974. *Families and family therapy.* Cambridge, MA: Harvard University Press.

Seashore, S.E., and Yuchtman, E. 1968. The elements of organizational performance. In *People, groups and organizations.*, ed. B. Indik, and F.K. Berrien.

Sonnenschien, P. 1981. Parents and professionals: An uneasy relationship. *Teaching Exceptional Children* 14 (2): 62–65.

Taylor, D.A., and Alpert, S.W. 1982. *Continuity and support following residential treatment.* New York: Child Welfare League of America.

Whittaker, J.K. 1979. *Caring for troubled children: Residential treatment in a community context.* San Francisco, CA: Jossey-Bass.

———. 1981. Family involvement in residential care: A support system for biological parents. In *The challenge of partnership: Working with parents in foster care.*, ed. A.N. Maluccio and P. Sinanoglu, 67–89. New York: Child Welfare League of America.

———. 1985. Family Matters: An Emergent Agenda. *Journal of Child Care* 2 (4): 11–26.

Youth Protection Act, Chapter P-34.1, Editeur Officiel du Quebec, 1984.

Young Offenders Act, Chapter 110, July 7, 1982.